This special 50th Anniversary Edition is dedicated to all those professional and aspiring amateur mixologists throughout the world who seek the most authoritative, accurate, and complete source for perfect drinks.

Mr. BOSTON

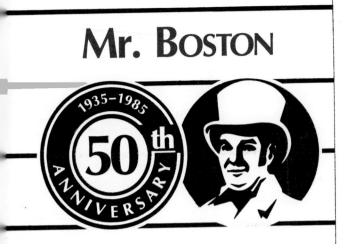

50th Anniversary Edition

Official

Bartender's

Guide

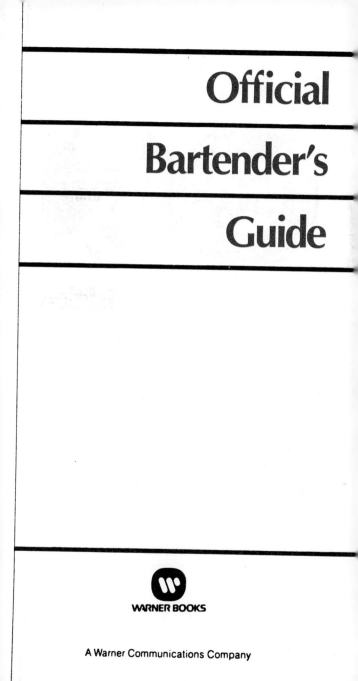

WARNER BOOKS

A Warner Communications Company

Acknowledgments

Appreciation is acknowledged to Leo Cotton, who served as editor of the original *Mr. Boston Bartender's Guide* which was first published in 1935. He continued as editor through the 49th printing—a period of over thirty-five years.

Further appreciation and acknowledgment is extended to: Fredda Isaacson, Editor, Warner Books; William J. Cummings, Art director; Joyce Goldsmith, Photography, Kinetic Corporation, Louisville, Kentucky; Andrius Balukas, Book Design, Amber Graphics, New York, New York; Robert Marinelli, Illustration; Roland Grybauskas, Book Marketing and Development, Publishers Marketing Associates.

Mr. Boston 50th Anniversary Bartender's Guide
Copyright © 1984 by Glenmore Distilleries Company

Material from Mr. Boston Bartender's Guide, copyright © 1935, 1936, 1940, 1941, 1946, 1948, 1949, 1951, 1953, 1955, 1957, 1959, 1960, 1961, 1962, 1963, 1964, 1965, 1966, 1967, 1968, 1969, 1970, 1974, 1976, 1977, 1978, 1979, 1981 by Mr. Boston Distiller Corporation.

Warner Books, Inc., 666 Fifth Avenue, New York, NY 10103
Ⓦ A Warner Communication Company

Printed in the United States of America
First Printing: November 1984
10 9 8 7 6 5 4 3 2 1

Design by Andrius Balukas
Illustrations by Robert Marinelli

Library of Congress Cataloging in Publication Data
Main entry under title:

Mr. Boston official 50th anniversary bartender's guide.

    Includes index.
 • 1. Liquors.   2. Cocktails.   3. Alcoholic beverages.
I. Title: Mr. Boston fiftieth anniversary bartender's
guide.   II. Title: 50th anniversary bartender's guide.
III. Title: Fiftieth anniversary bartender's guide.
TX951.M7   1984   641.8'74   84-11824
ISBN 0-446-38089-X (U.S.A.) (pbk.)
        0-446-38090-3 (Canada) (pbk.)

CONTENTS

INTRODUCTION

Welcome. You are holding in your hands the 50th Anniversary Edition of the first definitive guide to mixing perfect drinks. The *Mr. Boston Bartender's Guide* has been the official manual of bartenders and spirits professionals since it was first published in 1935. It has been endorsed, consulted, and considered a basic tool for bartenders for decades. In fact, over nine million copies have been sold since it first appeared shortly after the repeal of Prohibition as an urgently needed source of answers to questions such as: "How much is a dash? A lacing? Three parts? How do you frost glasses?"

Even experienced bartenders had trouble making the same drink taste the same way each time they mixed it. So Mr. Boston collected the best known and loved drink recipes, tested and standardized the measurements, and presented, in alphabetical order, recipes with such clear, easy-to-follow directions that, at last, anyone could be an expert at cocktail time.

Of course the book was copied. But originators stay original. With this, our 50th Anniversary Edition, we not only have updated our comprehensive spirits definition but we present for the first time an equally clear glossary to the most popular wines, beers, and liqueurs of the world. With this book as your guide, you can look at almost any wine label from any country and know exactly what you are buying, what the wine will taste like, where it is from, and what foods it complements. You will know how to store and serve wine and beer and a bit about the process and unique conditions that produced them.

None of this is stuffy or complicated. Spirits are meant to go with good times and good friends. So is the *Mr. Boston Bartender's Guide.* Informative but fun to read, complete but concise, it is the only book you need to make memorable drinks for your parties and perfect wine choices for intimate or elegant occasions.

So congratulations! You have made an excellent selection to enhance your expertise as a professional bartender or a well-informed host. Simply turn the page and you are on your way to making your friends'—and your own—favorite drinks superbly.

Blackberry Brandy straight-up

THE BASIC BAR: SUPPLIES AND METHODS

Since the repeal of Prohibition in 1933, *Mr. Boston Bartender's Guides* have passed down the secrets of mixing the perfect drink. This newly revised edition now contains over a thousand recipes, including many new cocktail recipes, made easily accessible by fingertip indexing.

The winning methods are gathered here for you to use with complete confidence. You need only follow this advice to achieve the extra artistry that will mark you as a professional.

There are a few practical rules to follow for stocking your bar and mixing drinks. You'll want to be able to satisfy the tastes of your guests quickly, so that you can enjoy the conviviality of good spirits. Following, you'll find the supplies you'll need to keep on hand to take care of anyone after a long, dusty day. And with the mastery of a few simple techniques carefully explained here, you'll find it easy to concoct quickly any drink calling for mixing, mashing, muddling, or simple stirring.

Equipment

The right tools make the job easier. For home or professional bar you'll need to have handy:

1. Can and bottle openers
2. Easy-to-use corkscrew
3. Traditional corkscrew
4. Glass stirring rod or long spoon
5. Coil-rimmed bar strainer
6. A tall, heavy-duty mixing glass or shaker
7. Small, sharp paring knife for cutting fruit or for shearing off rind
8. Wooden muddler or the back of a large wooden spoon for mashing herbs, fruit, etc.
9. Large pitcher
10. Fruit juice extractor
11. Set of measuring spoons
12. A jigger measure with easy-to-read half- and quarter-ounce measures
13. Ice bucket and ice tongs

Electric blender (optional)
Glassware

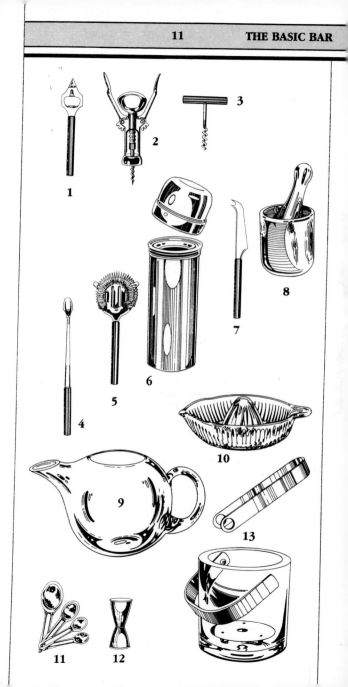

1

2

3

4

5

6

7

8

9

10

11

12

13

Glassware

The best glasses should be thin-lipped, transparent, and sound off in high registers when "pinged." Clean, sparkling glasses show off good drinks to great advantage. The proper glass enhances a drink. Here are illustrations of the basic glasses you will need, but you may find variations you prefer. Beside each recipe in the recipe section are line drawings of the classic shape used for each drink.

You might also need a coffee cup, coffee mug, or punch cup for some of the recipes.

Glass Name

1. Delmonico
2. Collins
3. Whiskey
4. Highball
5. Old Fashioned

6. Beer Mug
7. Beer Pilsner
8. Irish Cofee Cup
9. Pousse-Café
10. Parfait

11. Flip
12. Red Wine
13. White Wine
14. Sherry
15. Fluted Champagne

16. Brandy Snifter
17. Cocktail
18. Whiskey Sour
19. Cordial or Pony

Stocking a Bar

If you keep a 750-milliliter bottle of each of the spirits mentioned here, you'll be able to create just about any combination of drinks and *that* should satisfy just about everybody.

- Gin
- Vodka
- Rum (Light and Dark)
- Bourbon
- Scotch
- Tequilla
- Vermouth (Sweet and Dry)
- Red and White Wine
- Brandy, Port, Sherry
- Any assortment of Liqueurs popular in your crowd

When you want to get fancier you can diversify the standards with sophisticated variations: Irish as well as Scotch whiskey; Puerto Rican as well as Jamaican rum, etc. Time, experience, and your most frequent guests' tastes will shape your bar offerings.

Choose a selection of mixers from the following:

Colas
Ginger Ale
Club Soda or Seltzer
Tonic or Quinine Water
Lemon/Lime Sodas
Fresh fruit juices, especially:
    Orange, grapefruit, lemon, lime
Canned juices: Tomato, pineapple, cranberry
Sugar syrup (See p. 15 for recipe)
Water (in a small pitcher)

To garnish you'll need: `

- Jar of cocktail onions
- Jar of stuffed olives
- Lemons
- Limes
- Oranges
- Strawberries
- Celery stalks
- Bananas (for Banana Daiquiries)
- Bitters
- Cassis (Black Currant Syrup)
- Cinnamon sticks (for hot, mulled wines)
- Mint leaves (If you're into juleps)
- Tabasco sauce
- Worcestershire sauce
- Horseradish
- Maraschino cherries.
- Cucumber
- Pineapple

Certain fancy tropical-type drinks require these exotic additions to your potable collections:

Coconut milk
Grenadine syrup—Made from Pomegranates
Orange flower water—(or substitute Mr. Boston
   Triple Sec)
Orgeat syrup—Almond flavor syrup
Papaya juice
Passion fruit juice
Raspberry syrup
Light cream
Heavy cream
Whipping cream

You'll also need: Salt, pepper, granulated sugar, and powdered sugar.

To Make Simple Syrup or Sugar Syrup
In saucepan, gradually stir one pound granulated sugar into 13 oz. hot water to make 16 oz. simple syrup.

About Bitters

A little goes a long way. Made from numerous and intricate combinations of growing things (roots, barks, berries, and herbs) which are each uniquely flavored, they add zest to mixed drinks.

Angostura Bitters—Made from a Trinidadian secret recipe.

Abbott's Aged Bitters—Made in Baltimore since 1865.

Peychaud's Bitters—These come from New Orleans.

Orange Bitters—Made from the dried peel of mouthpuckering Seville oranges and sold by several English firms.

Vermouth

Vermouth is a white appetizer wine flavored with as many as thirty to forty different herbs, roots, berries, flowers, and seeds. There are nearly as many vermouth formulas as there are brand labels.

The dry variety (French) is light gold in color and has a delightful nutty flavor. Sweet (Italian) vermouth is red, richer in flavor, and more syrupy. Both are perishable and will lose their freshness if left too long in an opened bottle. Use with care and discretion in mixed drinks—be sure to follow the recipe since most people now prefer "drier" cocktails.

Ice

Bar ice must be clean and fresh and free of any flavor save water. If necessary, use bottled spring water.

Rule of thumb: You will always need more ice than you have. So buy extra and expect to make an ice run anyway.

Ice goes in the cocktail glass first. That way the spirits get cooled on the way in without any unnecessary splashing. Ice can be crushed, shaved, cracked, or cubed depending on the drink. If you can store only one kind of ice, buy cubes. Most highballs, old-fashioneds, and on-the-rocks drinks call for ice cubes. Use cracked or cubed ice for stirring and shaking; crushed or shaved ice for special tall drinks, frappes, and other drinks to be sipped through straws.

Techniques

How to Chill a Glass

Always chill before you fill. There are three ways to make a cocktail glass cold:

1.) Put the glasses in the refrigerator or freezer a couple of hours before using them.
2.) Fill the glasses with crushed ice just before using.
3.) Fill the glasses with cracked ice and stir it around before pouring in the drink.

If refrigerator space is not available for pre-chilling, fill each glass with ice before mixing. When the drink is ready, empty the glass, shake out all of the melted ice, and then pour in the drink.

How to Frost a Glass

There are two types of "frosted" glass. For "frosted" drinks, glasses should be stored in a refrigerator or buried in shaved ice long enough to give each glass a white, frosted, ice-cold look and feel.

For a "sugar-frosted" glass, moisten the rim of a pre-chilled glass with a slice of lime or lemon and then dip the rim into powdered sugar.

For Margaritas, rub the rim of the glass with a lime, invert glass, and dip into coarse salt.

How to Muddle

Muddling is a simple mashing technique for grinding herbs such as mint smooth in the bottom of a glass. You can buy a wooden muddler in a bar supply store. It crushes the herbs, much as the back of a soup spoon might, without scarring your glassware.

To Stir or Not to Stir

Pitchers of cocktails need at least ten seconds of stirring to mix properly. Carbonated mixers in drinks do much of their own stirring just by naturally bubbling. Two stirs from you will complete the job.

When to Shake

Shake any drink made with juices, sugar, eggs, or cream, or use an electric blender. Strain cocktails from shaker or blender to a glass through a coil rimmer strainer.

Pouring

Pour drinks as soon as you make them or they will wilt. Leftovers should be discarded or they will be too diluted by the time you get to "seconds."

When making a batch of drinks at once, set up the glasses in a row. Pour until each glass is half full, then backtrack until the shaker is empty. That way everyone gets the same amount, thoroughly mixed.

Floating Liqueurs

To create a rainbow effect in a glass with different colored cordials requires a special pouring technique. Simply pour each liqueur slowly over an inverted teaspoon (rounded side up) into a glass. Start with the heaviest liqueur first. (Recipes will give proper order). Pour *slowly*.

The rounded surface of the spoon will spread each liqueur over the one beneath without mixing them. You can accomplish the same trick using a glass rod. Pour slowly down the rod.

The Secret of Flaming

The secret to setting brandy (or other high alcohol spirits) aflame is first to warm it and its glass until almost hot. You can warm a glass by holding it by its stem above the flame or electric coil on your stove until the glass feels warm. (Avoid touching the glass to the flame or coil which could char or crack the glass).

Next, heat some brandy in a saucepan above the flame (or in a cooking pan). When the brandy is hot, ignite it with a match. If it's hot enough it will flame instantly. Pour the flaming liquid carefully into the other brandy you want flamed. If all the liquid is warm enough it will ignite.

Warning: Flames can shoot high suddenly. Look up and be sure there's nothing "en route" that can ignite. That includes your hair. Have an open box of baking soda handy in case of accidents. Pour it over flames to extinguish them. Use pot holders to protect your hands from the hot glass, spoon, or pan.

When Using Eggs

Eggs go into the shaker before the liquor (so that you can make sure the egg is fresh). To separate yolk from white, crack the egg in half on the edge of a glass. Pour the egg yolk from one half-shell to the other, back and forth, until the white runs down into the glass below and only the yolk is left in the shell.

Use cracked ice to blend egg with other ingredients you need chilled.

Using Fruit and Fruit Juices

Whenever possible use only *fresh* fruit. Wash the outside peel before using. Fruit can be cut in wedges or in slices. If slices are used, they should be cut about one-quarter-inch thick and slit toward the center to fix slice on rim of glass. Make sure garnishes are fresh and cold.

When mixing drinks containing fruit juices, *always* pour

the liquor last. Squeeze and strain fruit juices just before using to insure freshness and good taste. Avoid artificial, concentrated substitutes.

When recipes call for a twist of lemon peel, rub a narrow strip of peel around the rim of the glass to deposit the oil on it. Then twist the peel so that the oil (usually one small drop) will drop into the drink. Then drop in the peel. The lemon oil gives added character to the cocktail which many prefer.

To Open Champagne or Sparkling Wine

When the bottle is well chilled, wrap it in a clean white towel and undo the wire around the cork. Pointing the bottle away from people and priceless objects, hold the cork with one hand, grasp the bottle by the indentation on the bottom and slowly turn the bottle (not the cork!) until the cork comes free with a pop! Pour slowly into the center of the glass.

To Open Wine

Cut the seal around the neck with a sharp knife just below the top. Peel off neatly, exposing the cork. Insert the corkscrew and turn until the corkscrew is completely inside the cork. With a steady pull, remove cork. If the cork crumbles or breaks, pour the wine through a tea strainer when serving. Or decant through a strainer into another container for serving.

AMERICA'S FAVORITE DRINKS

Gin and Tonic, Screwdriver, Margarita and Bloody Mary

Black Russian, Collins, Daiquiri, Manhattan, and Whiskey Sour

BLACK RUSSIAN
- 1$\frac{1}{2}$ oz.   Mr. Boston Vodka
- $\frac{3}{4}$ oz.   Mr. Boston Coffee Flavored Brandy

Pour over ice cubes in old-fashioned cocktail glass.

BLOODY MARY
- 1$\frac{1}{2}$ oz.   Mr. Boston Vodka
- 3 oz.   Tomato Juice
- 1 dash   Lemon Juice
- $\frac{1}{2}$ tsp.   Worcestershire Sauce
- 2 or 3 drops Tabasco Sauce
- Pepper and Salt

Shake with ice and strain into old-fashioned glass over ice cubes. A wedge of lime may be added.

BRANDY ALEXANDER
- $\frac{1}{2}$ oz.   Mr. Boston Crème de Cacao (Brown)
- $\frac{1}{2}$ oz.   Mr. Boston Five Star Brandy
- $\frac{1}{2}$ oz.   Heavy Cream

Shake well with cracked ice and strain into a cocktail glass.

DAIQUIRI
- Juice of 1 Lime
- 1 tsp.   Powdered Sugar
- 1$\frac{1}{2}$ oz.   Mr. Boston Rum

Shake with ice and strain into cocktail glass.

GIMLET

1 oz.   Rose's Lime Juice
1 tsp.   Powdered Sugar
1 1/2 oz.   Mr. Boston Gin
Shake with ice and strain into cocktail glass.

GIN and TONIC

2 oz.   Mr. Boston Gin
Tonic
Pour gin into highball glass over ice cubes and fill with tonic water. Stir.

MANHATTAN

3/4 oz.   Sweet Vermouth
1 1/2 oz.   Old Thompson Blended Whiskey
Stir with ice and strain into cocktail glass. Serve with a cherry.

MARGARITA

1 1/2 oz.   Gavilan Tequila
1/2 oz.   Mr. Boston Triple Sec
1 oz.   Lemon or Lime Juice
Rub rim of cocktail glass with rind of lemon or lime, dip rim in salt. Shake ingredients with ice and strain into the salt-rimmed glass.

MARTINI

See Special Martini Section on pages 204 and 206.

PIÑA COLADA

3 oz.   Mr. Boston Rum
3 tbsp.   Coconut Milk
3 tbsp.   Crushed Pineapple
Place in an electric blender with two cups of crushed ice and blend at high speed for a short time. Strain into collins glass and serve with straw.

SCREWDRIVER

Put two or three cubes of ice into highball glass. Add 2 oz. Mr. Boston Vodka. Fill balance of glass with orange juice and stir.

TEQUILA SUNRISE

2 oz.   Gavilan Tequila
4 oz.   Orange Juice
3/4 oz.   Grenadine
Stir tequila and orange juice with ice and strain into highball glass. Add ice cubes. Pour in grenadine slowly and allow to settle. Before drinking, stir to complete your sunrise.

TOM COLLINS

Juice of $\frac{1}{2}$ Lemon
1 tsp.   Powdered Sugar
2 oz.   Mr. Boston Gin

Shake with ice and strain into collins glass. Add several ice cubes, fill with carbonated water, and stir. Decorate with slices of lemon, orange, and a cherry. Serve with straw.

WHISKEY SOUR

Juice of $\frac{1}{2}$ Lemon
$\frac{1}{2}$ tsp.   Powdered Sugar
2 oz.   Old Thompson Blended Whiskey

Shake with ice and strain into sour glass. Decorate with a half-slice of lemon and a cherry.

Martini, Brandy Alexander, Tequila Sunrise, Gimlet, and Piña Colada

Amaretto di Saronno straight-up and on-the-rocks

A

ABBEY COCKTAIL
1¹/₂ oz. Mr. Boston Gin
Juice of ¹/₄ Orange
1 dash Orange Bitters
Shake with ice and strain
into cocktail glass. Add a
maraschino cherry.

ABSINTHE COCKTAIL
1¹/₂ oz. Absinthe
  Substitute
2 tbsp. Water
1¹/₂ tsp. Mr. Boston
  Anisette
1 dash Orange Bitters
Shake with ice and strain
into cocktail glass.

ABSINTHE DRIP
COCKTAIL
1¹/₂ oz. Absinthe
  Substitute
1 Sugar Cube
Pour absinthe substitute
into special drip glass or
old-fashioned cocktail glass.
Place sugar cube over hole
of drip spoon (or in silver
tea strainer). Pack spoon or
strainer with cracked ice,
pour cold water to fill.
When water has dripped
through, drink is ready.

ABSINTHE SPECIAL
COCKTAIL
1¹/₂ oz. Absinthe
  Substitute
1 oz. Water
¹/₄ tsp. Powdered Sugar
1 dash Orange Bitters
Shake with ice and strain
into cocktail glass.

ACAPULCO
1¹/₂ oz. Mr. Boston Rum
1 tbsp. Lime Juice
1¹/₂ tsp. Mr. Boston
  Triple Sec
1 tsp. Sugar
1 Egg White
Combine and shake all
ingredients with ice and
strain into old-fashioned
glass over ice cubes. Add a
sprig of mint.

ADAM AND EVE
1 oz.   Forbidden Fruit
1 oz.   Mr. Boston Gin
1 oz.   Mr. Boston Five
  Star Brandy
1 dash Lemon Juice
Shake well with cracked ice
and strain into cocktail
glass.

ADONIS COCKTAIL
1 dash Orange Bitters
$^3/_4$ oz. Sweet Vermouth
1$^1/_2$ oz. Dry Sherry
Stir with ice and strain into cocktail glass.

AFFAIR
2 oz. Mr. Boston Original Strawberry Schnapps
2 oz. Cranberry Juice
2 oz. Orange Juice
Pour over ice in a highball glass and top wth club soda if desired.

AFFINITY COCKTAIL
1 oz. Dry Vermouth
1 oz. Sweet Vermouth
1 oz. Desmond & Duff Scotch
3 dashes Orange Bitters
Stir with ice and strain into cocktail glass.

AFTER DINNER COCKTAIL
1 oz. Mr. Boston Apricot Flavored Brandy
1 oz. Mr. Boston Triple Sec
Juice of 1 Lime
Shake with ice and strain into cocktail glass. Leave lime in glass.

AFTER SUPPER COCKTAIL
1 oz. Mr. Boston Apricot Flavored Brandy
1 oz. Mr. Boston Triple Sec
$^1/_2$ tsp. Lemon Juice
Shake with ice and strain into cocktail glass.

A.J.
1$^1/_2$ oz. Applejack
1 oz. Grapefruit Juice
Shake with ice and strain into cocktail glass.

ALABAMA FIZZ
Juice of $^1/_2$ Lemon
1 tsp. Powdered Sugar
2 oz. Mr. Boston Gin
Shake well with cracked ice and strain into highball glass over two ice cubes. Fill with carbonated water. Add two sprigs of fresh mint.

ALABAMA SLAMMER
1 oz. Amaretto di Saronno
1 oz. Southern Comfort
$^1/_2$ oz. Mr. Boston Sloe Gin
Stir in a highball glass over ice and add a splash of lemon juice.

ALASKA COCKTAIL
2 dashes Orange Bitters
1$^1/_2$ oz. Mr. Boston Gin
$^3/_4$ oz. Chartreuse (Yellow)
Stir with ice and strain into cocktail glass.

ALBEMARLE FIZZ

Juice of $\frac{1}{2}$ Lemon
1 tsp.   Powdered Sugar
2 oz.   Mr. Boston Gin
1 tsp.   Raspberry Syrup

Shake with ice and strain into highball glass over two ice cubes. Fill with carbonated water.

ALEXANDER COCKTAIL NO. 1

1 oz.   Mr. Boston Gin
1 oz.   Mr. Boston Crème de Cacao (White)
1 oz.   Light Cream

Shake with ice and strain into cocktail glass. Sprinkle nutmeg on top.

ALEXANDER COCKTAIL NO. 2

1 oz.   Mr. Boston Crème de Cacao (White)
1 oz.   Mr. Boston Five Star Brandy
1 oz.   Light Cream

Shake with ice and strain into cocktail glass. Sprinkle nutmeg on top.

ALEXANDER'S SISTER COCKTAIL

1 oz.   Mr. Boston Dry Gin
1 oz.   Mr. Boston Crème de Menthe (Green)
1 oz.   Light Cream

Shake with ice and strain into cocktail glass. Sprinkle nutmeg on top.

ALFIE COCKTAIL

$1\frac{1}{2}$ oz. Mr. Boston Lemon Vodka
1 tbsp.   Pineapple Juice
1 dash Mr. Boston Triple Sec

Shake with ice and strain into cocktail glass.

ALGONQUIN

$1\frac{1}{2}$ oz. Old Thompson Blended Whiskey
1 oz.   Dry Vermouth
1 oz.   Pineapple Juice

Shake with ice and strain into cocktail glass.

ALLEGHENY

1 oz.   Kentucky Tavern Bourbon
1 oz.   Dry Vermouth
$1\frac{1}{2}$ tsp. Mr. Boston Blackberry Flavored Brandy
$1\frac{1}{2}$ tsp. Lemon Juice

Shake with ice and strain into cocktail glass. Add a twist of lemon peel on top.

ALLEN COCKTAIL

$1\frac{1}{2}$ tsp. Lemon Juice
$\frac{3}{4}$ oz.   Maraschino
$1\frac{1}{2}$ oz. Mr. Boston Gin

Shake with ice and strain into cocktail glass.

ALLIES COCKTAIL

1 oz.   Dry Vermouth
1 oz.   Mr. Boston Gin
$\frac{1}{2}$ tsp. Kümmel

Stir with ice and strain into cocktail glass.

ALMERIA

1½ oz. Mr. Boston Rum
1 oz.   Mr. Boston
  Coffee Flavored Brandy
1 Egg White

Shake all ingredients with cracked ice and strain into cocktail glass.

AMARETTO AND CREAM

1½ oz. Amaretto di
  Saronno
1½ oz. Light Cream

Shake well with cracked ice. Strain and serve in cocktail glass.

AMARETTO SOUR

1½ oz. Amaretto di
  Saronno
¾ oz. Lemon Juice (No
  Sugar)

Shake well with cracked ice and strain into sour glass. Garnish with a slice of orange.

AMARETTO STINGER

1½ oz. Amaretto di
  Saronno
¾ oz. Mr. Boston
  Crème de Menthe
  (White)

Shake well with ice. Strain and serve in cocktail glass.

AMBASSADOR'S MORNING LIFT

32 oz. Prepared Dairy
  Eggnog
6 oz. Cognac
3 oz. Jamaica Rum
3 oz. Mr. Boston
  Crème de Cacao
  (Brown)

Combine in large punch bowl and serve. Mr. Boston Five Star Brandy or Kentucky Tavern Bourbon may be substituted for cognac.

AMBROSIA

1 oz. Applejack
1 oz. Mr. Boston Five
  Star Brandy
1 dash Mr. Boston Triple
  Sec
Juice of 1 Lemon
Shadow Creek
  Champagne

Shake all ingredients except champagne. Pour contents into highball glass with cubed ice. Fill with champagne.

AMERICAN BEAUTY COCKTAIL

1 tbsp. Orange Juice
1 tbsp. Grenadine
½ oz. Dry Vermouth
½ oz. Mr. Boston Five
  Star Brandy
¼ tsp. Mr. Boston
  Crème de Menthe
  (White)

Shake with ice and strain into cocktail glass and top with a dash of port.

AMERICAN GROG
🍬 1 lump Sugar
Juice of ¹/₄ Lemon
1¹/₂ oz. Mr. Boston Rum
Pour ingredients into hot mug and fill with hot water. Stir.

AMERICANO
2 oz. Sweet Vermouth
2 oz. Campari
Carbonated Water
Pour sweet vermouth and Campari into highball glass over ice cubes. Fill with carbonated water and stir. Add a twist of lemon peel.

AMER PICON COCKTAIL
Juice of 1 Lime
1 tsp. Grenadine
1¹/₂ oz. Amer Picon
Shake with ice and strain into cocktail glass.

ANDALUSIA
1¹/₂ oz. Dry Sherry
¹/₂ oz. Mr. Boston Five Star Brandy
¹/₂ oz. Mr. Boston Rum
Stir well with cracked ice and strain into cocktail glass.

ANGEL FACE
1 oz. Mr. Boston Gin
¹/₂ oz. Mr. Boston Apricot Flavored Brandy
¹/₂ oz. Mr. Boston Apple Brandy
Shake well with cracked ice and strain into cocktail glass.

ANGEL'S DELIGHT
1¹/₂ tsp. Grenadine
1¹/₂ tsp. Mr. Boston Triple Sec
1¹/₂ tsp. Mr. Boston Sloe Gin
1¹/₂ tsp. Light Cream
Pour carefully, in order given, into pousse-café glass so that each ingredient floats on preceding one without mixing.

ANGEL'S KISS
¹/₄ oz. Mr. Boston Crème de Cacao (White)
¹/₄ oz. Mr. Boston Sloe Gin
¹/₄ oz. Mr. Boston Five Star Brandy
¹/₄ oz. Light Cream
Pour ingredients carefully, in order given, so that they do not mix. Use pousse-café glass.

ANGEL'S TIP
³/₄ oz. Mr. Boston Crème de Cacao (White)
¹/₄ oz. Light Cream
Float cream and insert toothpick in cherry and put on top. Use pousse-café glass.

ANGEL'S WING
- 1/2 oz. Mr. Boston
  Crème de Cacao
  (White)
  1/2 oz. Mr. Boston Five
  Star Brandy
  1 tbsp. Light Cream

Pour ingredients carefully, in order given, so that they do not mix. Use pousse-café glass.

ANGLER'S COCKTAIL
- 2 dashes Bitters
  3 dashes Orange Bitters
  1 1/2 oz. Mr. Boston Gin
  1 dash Grenadine

Shake with cracked ice and pour into old-fashioned glass over ice cubes.

ANTE
- 1 oz. Mr. Boston Apple
  Brandy
  1/2 oz. Mr. Boston Triple
  Sec
  1 oz. Dubonnet®

Stir well with cracked ice and strain into cocktail glass.

ANTOINE SPECIAL
- 1 1/2 oz. Dubonnet®
  1 1/2 oz. Dry Vermouth

Float vermouth on top of chilled Dubonnet® in a wine glass.

APPLE BLOW FIZZ
- 1 Egg White
  Juice of 1/2 Lemon
  1 tsp. Powdered Sugar
  2 oz. Mr. Boston Apple
  Brandy

Shake with ice and strain into highball glass with two ice cubes. Fill with carbonated water.

APPLE BRANDY COCKTAIL
- 1 1/2 oz. Mr. Boston Apple
  Brandy
  1 tsp. Grenadine
  1 tsp. Lemon Juice

Shake with ice and strain into cocktail glass.

APPLE BRANDY HIGHBALL
- 2 oz. Mr. Boston Apple
  Brandy

Pour over ice cubes in a highball glass. Fill with ginger ale or carbonated water. Add a twist of lemon peel, if desired, and stir.

APPLE BRANDY RICKEY
- Juice of 1/2 Lime
  1 1/2 oz. Mr. Boston Apple
  Brandy

Fill highball glass with carbonated water and ice cubes. Leave lime in glass. Stir.

APPLE BRANDY SOUR

Juice of 1/2 Lemon
1/2 tsp. Powdered Sugar
2 oz. Mr. Boston Apple
Brandy

Shake with ice and strain into sour glass. Decorate with a half-slice of lemon and a cherry.

APPLECAR

1 oz. Applejack
1 oz. Mr. Boston Triple Sec
1 oz. Lemon Juice

Shake with ice and strain into cocktail glass.

APPLE COLADA

2 oz. Mr. Boston Apple Schnapps
1 oz. Cream of Coconut
1 oz. Half-and-Half

Blend all ingredients with two cups of crushed ice in an electric blender at a high speed. Pour into a tall glass and serve with a straw. Garnish with an apple slice and cherry.

APPLEJACK PUNCH

1.75 Liter Applejack
4 oz. Grenadine
16 oz. Orange Juice

Combine ingredients in punch bowl with large block of ice. Add 64 oz. ginger ale and slices of apple.

APPLE PIE NO. 1

3/4 oz. Mr. Boston Rum
3/4 oz. Sweet Vermouth
1 tsp. Mr. Boston Apple Brandy
1/2 tsp. Grenadine
1 tsp. Lemon Juice

Shake with ice and strain into cocktail glass.

APPLE PIE NO. 2

3 oz. Mr. Boston Apple Schnapps
Splash Mr. Boston Cinnamon Schnapps

Pour over ice and garnish with an apple slice and sprinkle with cinnamon.

APPLE RUM RICKEY

3/4 oz. Applejack
3/4 oz. Mr. Boston Rum
1/4 Lime

Pour applejack and rum into highball glass over ice cubes. Fill with carbonated water. Squeeze lime and drop into glass. Stir.

APRICOT ANISE COLLINS

1 1/2 oz. Mr. Boston Gin
1/2 oz. Mr. Boston Apricot Flavored Brandy
1 1/2 tsp. Mr. Boston Anisette
1 tbsp. Lemon Juice

Shake with ice and strain into collins glass over ice. Fill with carbonated water and stir lightly. Garnish with a slice of lemon.

APRICOT BRANDY RICKEY

Juice of 1/2 Lime
2 oz. Mr. Boston Apricot Flavored Brandy

Pour into highball glass over ice cubes and fill with carbonated water. Drop a rind of lime into glass. Stir.

APRICOT COCKTAIL

Juice of 1/4 Lemon
Juice of 1/4 Orange
1 1/2 oz. Mr. Boston Apricot Flavored Brandy
1 tsp. Mr. Boston Gin

Shake with ice and strain into cocktail glass.

APRICOT COOLER

1/2 tsp. Powdered Sugar
2 oz. Carbonated Water
2 oz. Mr. Boston Apricot Flavored Brandy

In a collins glass, dissolve powdered sugar and carbonated water. Stir and fill glass with cracked ice and add brandy.
Fill with carbonated water or ginger ale and stir again. Insert a spiral of orange or lemon peel (or both) and dangle end over rim of glass.

APRICOT FIZZ

Juice of 1/2 Lemon
Juice of 1/2 Lime
1 tsp. Powdered Sugar
2 oz. Mr. Boston Apricot Flavored Brandy

Shake with cracked ice and strain into highball glass with two ice cubes. Fill with carbonated water.

APRICOT LADY

1 1/4 oz. Mr. Boston Rum
1 oz. Mr. Boston Apricot Flavored Brandy
1/4 tsp. Mr. Boston Triple Sec
1 tbsp. Lime Juice
1 Egg White

Shake all ingredients with ice and strain into old-fashioned glass over ice cubes. Add an orange slice.

APRIHOT
3 oz.   Mr. Boston Apricot Flavored Brandy
3 oz.   Boiling Water
Combine in coffee mug with a dash of cinnamon, and garnish with an orange or lemon slice.

AQUARIUS
1½ oz. Old Thompson Blended Whiskey
½ oz.   Mr. Boston Cherry Flavored Brandy
1 oz.   Cranberry Juice
Shake with ice and strain into old-fashioned glass over ice.

AQUEDUCT
1½ oz. Mr. Boston Vodka
1½ tsp. Curaçao (White)
1½ tsp. Mr. Boston Apricot Flavored Brandy
1 tbsp. Lime Juice
Combine and shake all ingredients and strain into cocktail glass. Add a twist of orange peel.

ARISE MY LOVE
1 tsp.   Mr. Boston Crème de Menthe (Green)
Chilled Shadow Creek Champagne
Put crème de menthe into champagne glass. Fill with champagne.

ARTILLERY
1½ oz. Mr. Boston Gin
1½ tsp. Sweet Vermouth
2 dashes Bitters
Stir with ice and strain into cocktail glass.

AUNT JEMIMA
½ oz.   Mr. Boston Five Star Brandy
½ oz.   Mr. Boston Crème de Cacao (White)
½ oz.   Benedictine
Pour carefully, in order given, into a pousse-café glass so that ingredients do not mix.

B

B & B
▽ 1/2 oz. Benedictine
1/2 oz. Mr. Boston Five
      Star Brandy
Use cordial glass and
carefully float the brandy
on top of the Benedictine.

BABBIE'S SPECIAL
COCKTAIL
▽ 1 tbsp. Light Cream
1 1/2 oz. Mr. Boston
         Apricot Flavored
         Brandy
1/4 tsp. Mr. Boston Gin
Shake with ice and strain
into cocktail glass.

BACARDI COCKTAIL
▽ 1 1/2 oz. Bacardi Rum
Juice of 1/2 Lime
1/2 tsp. Grenadine
Shake with ice and strain
into cocktail glass.

BACHELOR'S BAIT
COCKTAIL
▽ 1 1/2 oz. Mr. Boston Gin
1 Egg White
1 dash Orange Bitters
1/2 tsp. Grenadine
Shake with ice and strain
into cocktail glass.

BALTIMORE BRACER
▽ 1 oz. Mr. Boston
       Anisette
1 oz. Mr. Boston Five
     Star Brandy
1 Egg White
Shake with ice and strain
into cocktail glass.

BALTIMORE EGGNOG
▽ 1 Whole Egg
1 tsp. Powdered Sugar
1 oz. Mr. Boston Five
     Star Brandy
1 oz. Jamaica Rum
1 oz. Madeira
3/4 cup Milk
Shake well with ice and
strain into collins glass.
Sprinkle nutmeg on top.

BAMBOO COCKTAIL
▽ 1 1/2 oz. Dry Sherry
3/4 oz. Dry Vermouth
1 dash Orange Bitters
Stir with ice and strain into
cocktail glass.

BANANA DAIQUIRI
Same as Frozen Daiquiri on
page 85 but add a sliced
medium-size ripe banana
before blending.

BANANA PUNCH

2 oz.   Mr. Boston Vodka
1½ tsp. Mr. Boston
    Apricot Flavored
    Brandy
Juice of ½ Lime
Pour into collins glass filled
with crushed ice. Add
carbonated water and top
with slices of banana and
sprigs of mint.

BANSHEE

1 oz.   Mr. Boston
    Crème de Banana
½ oz.   Mr. Boston
    Crème de Cacao
    (White)
½ oz.   Light Cream
Shake with cracked ice and
strain into cocktail glass.

BARBARY COAST

½ oz.   Mr. Boston Gin
½ oz.   Mr. Boston Rum
½ oz.   Mr. Boston White
    Crème de Cacao
½ oz.   Desmond & Duff
    Scotch
½ oz.   Light Cream
Shake with ice and strain
into cocktail glass.

BARNABY'S BUFFALO BLIZZARD*

1 oz.   Mr. Boston
    Crème de Cacao
    (White)
¾ oz.   Mr. Boston Vodka
1 oz.   Galliano
Vanilla Ice Cream
Dash Grenadine
Whipped Cream
¾ cup Milk
Shake or blend. Serve in a
collins glass.

BARON COCKTAIL

½ oz.   Dry Vermouth
1½ oz. Mr. Boston Gin
1½ tsp. Mr. Boston Triple
    Sec
½ tsp. Sweet Vermouth
Stir with ice and strain into
cocktail glass. Add a twist of
lemon peel.

BARTON SPECIAL

½ oz.   Applejack
¼ oz.   Desmond & Duff
    Scotch
¼ oz.   Mr. Boston Gin
Shake with ice and strain
into old-fashioned glass
over ice cubes.

BEACHCOMBER

1½ oz. Mr. Boston Rum
½ oz.   Lime Juice
½ oz.   Mr. Boston Triple
    Sec
1 dash Maraschino
Shake with cracked ice and
strain into cocktail glass
rimmed with lime juice and
sugar.

*Barnaby's Restaurant, Buffalo, N.Y.

BEADLESTONE COCKTAIL
- 1½ oz. Dry Vermouth
- 1½ oz. Desmond & Duff Scotch

Stir with ice and strain into cocktail glass.

BEALS COCKTAIL
- 1½ oz. Desmond & Duff Scotch
- ½ oz. Dry Vermouth
- ½ oz. Sweet Vermouth

Stir with ice and strain into cocktail glass.

BEAUTY SPOT COCKTAIL
- 1 tsp. Orange Juice
- ½ oz. Sweet Vermouth
- ½ oz. Dry Vermouth
- 1 oz. Mr. Boston Gin

Shake with ice and strain into cocktail glass, with a dash of grenadine in bottom of glass.

BEER BUSTER
- 1½ oz. Mr. Boston 100 proof Vodka
- Ice Cold Beer
- 2 dashes Tabasco Sauce

Put vodka in a highball glass and fill with beer or ale. Add tabasco and stir lightly.

BEE STINGER
Substitute Mr. Boston Blackberry Brandy for brandy in a Stinger, page 165.

BELMONT COCKTAIL
- 2 oz. Mr. Boston Gin
- 1 tsp. Raspberry Syrup
- ¾ oz. Light Cream

Shake with ice and strain into cocktail glass.

BENNETT COCKTAIL
- Juice of ½ Lime
- 1½ oz. Mr. Boston Gin
- ½ tsp. Powdered Sugar
- 2 dashes Orange Bitters

Shake with ice and strain into cocktail glass.

BENTLEY
- 1½ oz. Mr. Boston Apple Brandy
- 1 oz. Dubonnet®

Stir with cracked ice and strain into cocktail glass. Add a twist of lemon peel.

BERMUDA BOUQUET
- Juice of ¼ Orange
- Juice of ½ Lemon
- 1 tsp. Powdered Sugar
- 1½ oz. Mr. Boston Gin
- 1 oz. Mr. Boston Apricot Flavored Brandy
- 1 tsp. Grenadine
- ½ tsp. Mr. Boston Triple Sec

Shake with ice and strain into highball glass with ice cubes.

BERMUDA HIGHBALL

- ¾ oz. Mr. Boston Gin
- ¾ oz. Mr. Boston Five Star Brandy
- ¾ oz. Dry Vermouth

Pour into highball glass over ice cubes. Fill with ginger ale or carbonated water. Add a twist of lemon peel and stir.

BERMUDA ROSE

- 1¼ oz. Mr. Boston Gin
- 1½ tsp. Mr. Boston Apricot Flavored Brandy
- 1½ tsp. Grenadine

Shake with ice and strain into cocktail glass.

BETSY ROSS

- 1½ oz. Mr. Boston Five Star Brandy
- 1½ oz. Port
- 1 dash Mr. Boston Triple Sec

Stir with cracked ice and strain into cocktail glass.

BETWEEN-THE-SHEETS

- Juice of ¼ Lemon
- ½ oz. Mr. Boston Five Star Brandy
- ½ oz. Mr. Boston Triple Sec
- ½ oz. Mr. Boston Rum

Shake with ice and strain into cocktail glass.

BIFFY COCKTAIL

- Juice of ½ Lemon
- 1 tbsp. Swedish Punch
- 1½ oz. Mr. Boston Gin

Shake with ice and strain into cocktail glass.

BIJOU COCKTAIL

- ¾ oz. Mr. Boston Gin
- ¾ oz. Chartreuse (Green)
- ¾ oz. Sweet Vermouth
- 1 dash Orange Bitters

Stir with ice and strain into cocktail glass. Add a cherry on top.

BILLY TAYLOR

- Juice of ½ Lime
- 2 oz. Mr. Boston Gin

Fill collins glass with carbonated water and ice cubes. Stir.

BIRD-OF-PARADISE FIZZ

- Juice of ½ Lemon
- 1 tsp. Powdered Sugar
- 1 Egg White
- 1 tsp. Grenadine
- 2 oz. Mr. Boston Gin

Shake with ice and strain into highball glass over two ice cubes. Fill with carbonated water.

BISHOP

- Juice of ¼ Lemon
- Juice of ¼ Orange
- 1 tsp. Powdered Sugar

Shake with ice and strain into highball glass. Add two ice cubes, fill with burgundy and stir well. Decorate with fruits.

BITTERS HIGHBALL
- ¾ oz. Bitters
- Ginger Ale or Carbonated Water

Fill highball glass with bitters, ice cubes, and ginger ale or carbonated water. Add a twist of lemon peel, if desired, and stir.

BITTERSWEET
- 1½ oz. Sweet Vermouth
- 1½ oz. Dry Vermouth
- 1 dash Bitters
- 1 dash Orange Bitters

Stir with cracked ice and strain into cocktail glass. Add a twist of orange peel.

BLACK DEVIL
- 2 oz. Mr. Boston Rum
- ½ oz. Dry Vermouth

Stir with cracked ice and strain into cocktail glass. Add a black olive.

BLACK HAWK
- 1¼ oz. Old Thompson Blended Whiskey
- 1¼ oz. Mr. Boston Sloe Gin

Stir with ice and strain into cocktail glass. Serve with a cherry.

BLACKJACK
- 1 oz. Kirschwasser
- ½ oz. Mr. Boston Five Star Brandy
- 1 oz. Coffee

Shake with cracked ice and strain into old-fashioned glass over ice cubes.

BLACK MAGIC
- 1½ oz. Mr. Boston Vodka
- ¾ oz. Expresso® Coffee Liqueur
- 1 dash Lemon Juice

Stir and serve in old-fashioned glass over ice cubes and add a twist of lemon peel.

BLACK MARIA
- 2 oz. Mr. Boston Coffee Flavored Brandy
- 2 oz. Mr. Boston Rum
- 4 oz. Strong Black Coffee
- 2 tsp. Powdered Sugar

Stir in brandy snifter and add cracked ice.

BLACK RUSSIAN
- 1½ oz. Mr. Boston Vodka
- ¾ oz. Mr. Boston Coffee Flavored Brandy

Pour over ice cubes in old-fashioned cocktail glass.

BLACK SOMBRERO
See Sombrero recipe on page 162.

BLACKTHORN
- 1½ oz. Mr. Boston Sloe Gin
- 1 oz. Sweet Vermouth

Stir with ice and strain into cocktail glass. Add a twist of lemon peel.

BLACK VELVET

5 oz.   Chilled Stout
5 oz.   Chilled Shadow
        Creek Champagne

Pour very carefully, in order given, into champagne glass so that the stout and champagne don't mix.

BLANCHE

1 oz.   Mr. Boston
        Anisette
1 oz.   Mr. Boston Triple
        Sec
$^1/_2$ oz.   Curaçao (White)

Shake with cracked ice and strain into cocktail glass.

BLARNEY STONE COCKTAIL

2 oz.   Irish Whisky
$^1/_2$ tsp.   Absinthe
        Substitute
$^1/_2$ tsp.   Mr. Boston Triple
        Sec
$^1/_4$ tsp.   Maraschino
1 dash   Bitters

Shake with ice and strain into cocktail glass. Add a twist of orange peel and an olive.

BLOOD-AND-SAND COCKTAIL

1 tbsp.   Orange Juice
$^1/_2$ oz.   Desmond & Duff
          Scotch
$^1/_2$ oz.   Mr. Boston
          Cherry Flavored
          Brandy
$^1/_2$ oz.   Sweet Vermouth

Shake with ice and strain into cocktail glass.

BLOODHOUND COCKTAIL

$^1/_2$ oz.   Dry Vermouth
$^1/_2$ oz.   Sweet Vermouth
1 oz.   Mr. Boston Gin

Shake with ice and strain into cocktail glass. Decorate with two or three crushed strawberries.

BLOODY BULL

1 oz.   Gavilan Tequila
$^1/_2$ glass Tomato Juice
$^1/_2$ glass Beef Bouillon

Add all ingredients in a highball glass over ice. Stir and add a squeeze of lemon and a slice of lime.

BLOODY MARIA

1 oz.   Gavilan Tequila
2 oz.   Tomato Juice
1 dash   Lemon Juice
1 dash   Tabasco Sauce
1 dash   Celery Salt

Shake all ingredients with cracked ice. Strain into old-fashioned glass over ice cubes. Add a slice of lemon.

BLOODY MARY

1¹/₂ oz. Mr. Boston Vodka
3 oz.   Tomato Juice
1 dash Lemon Juice
¹/₂ tsp. Worcestershire
        Sauce
2 or 3 drops Tabasco
        Sauce
Pepper and Salt

Shake with ice and strain
into old-fashioned glass
over ice cubes. A wedge of
lime may be added.

BLUE BIRD

1¹/₂ oz. Mr. Boston Gin
¹/₂ oz. Mr. Boston Triple
        Sec
1 dash Bitters

Stir with ice cubes and
strain into cocktail glass.
Add a twist of lemon peel
and a cherry.

BLUE BLAZER

Use two large silver-plated
mugs, with handles.
2¹/₂ oz. Old Thompson
        Blended Whiskey
2¹/₂ oz. Boiling Water

Put the whiskey into one
mug, and the boiling water
into the other. Ignite the
whiskey and, while blazing,
mix both ingredients by
pouring them four or five
times from one mug to the
other. If done well, this will
have the appearance of a
continuous stream of liquid
fire. Sweeten with 1
teaspoon of powdered
sugar and serve with a twist
of lemon peel. Serve in a 4-
oz. hot whiskey glass.

BLUE DEVIL COCKTAIL

1 oz.   Mr. Boston Gin
Juice of ¹/₂ Lemon or 1
        Lime
1 tbsp. Maraschino
¹/₂ tsp. Blue Curaçao

Shake with ice and strain
into cocktail glass.

BLUE MONDAY COCKTAIL

1¹/₂ oz. Mr. Boston Vodka
³/₄ oz. Mr. Boston Triple
        Sec
1 dash Blue Food
        Coloring

Stir with ice and strain into
cocktail glass.

BLUE MOON COCKTAIL

1¹/₂ oz. Mr. Boston Gin
³/₄ oz. Blue Curaçao

Stir with ice and strain into
cocktail glass. Add a twist of
lemon peel.

BOBBY BURNS COCKTAIL

1¹/₂ oz. Sweet Vermouth
1¹/₂ oz. Desmond and
        Duff Scotch
1¹/₄ tsp. Benedictine

Stir with ice and strain into
cocktail glass. Add a twist of
lemon peel.

BOCCIE BALL

1¹/₂ oz. Amaretto di
        Saronno
1¹/₂ oz. Orange Juice
2 oz.   Club Soda

Serve in a highball glass
over ice.

Beer Buster

BOLERO

🍸 1 1/2 oz. Mr. Boston Rum
  3/4 oz. Mr. Boston Apple
    Brandy
  1/4 tsp. Sweet Vermouth
Stir well with cracked ice
and strain into cocktail
glass.

BOMBAY COCKTAIL

🍸 1/2 oz. Dry Vermouth
  1/2 oz. Sweet Vermouth
  1 oz. Mr. Boston Five
    Star Brandy
  1/4 tsp. Absinthe
    Substitute
  1/2 tsp. Mr. Boston Triple
    Sec
Stir with ice and strain into
cocktail glass.

BOMBAY PUNCH

🍶 Juice of 12 Lemons
Add enough powdered
sugar to sweeten. Pour over
a large block of ice in
punch bowl and stir. Then
add:
  32 oz. Mr. Boston Five
    Star Brandy
  32 oz. Dry Sherry
  1/2 cup Maraschino
  1/2 cup Mr. Boston Triple
    Sec
  4 750ml bottles Chilled
    Shadow Creek
    Champagne
  64 oz. Chilled
    Carbonated Water
Stir well and decorate with
fruits in season. Serve in
punch glasses.

BOOM BOOM PUNCH

🍶 64 oz. Mr. Boston Rum
  32 oz. Orange Juice
  1 750ml bottle Sweet
    Vermouth
  1 750ml bottle Chilled
    Shadow Creek
    Champagne
Pour into punch bowl over
large block of ice all
ingredients except
champagne. Stir. Add
champagne on top.
Decorate with sliced
bananas.

BOOMERANG

🍸 1 oz. Dry Vermouth
  1 1/2 oz. Mr. Boston Gin
  1 dash Bitters
  1 dash Maraschino
Stir with ice cubes and
strain into cocktail glass.
Add twist of lemon peel.

BORINQUEN

🥃 1 1/2 oz. Mr. Boston Rum
  1 tbsp. Passion Fruit
    Syrup
  1 oz. Lime Juice
  1 oz. Orange Juice
  1 tsp. 151 Proof Rum
Put half a cup of crushed
ice into blender. Add all
ingredients and blend at
low speed. Pour into old-
fashioned glass.

BOSOM CARESSER

1 oz. Mr. Boston Five
 Star Brandy
1 oz. Madeira
$^1/_2$ oz. Mr. Boston Triple
 Sec

Stir with cracked ice and
strain into cocktail glass.

BOSTON BULLET

See Special Martini Section
on pages 204 and 206.

BOSTON COCKTAIL

$^3/_4$ oz. Mr. Boston Gin
$^3/_4$ oz. Mr. Boston
 Apricot Flavored
 Brandy
Juice of $^1/_4$ Lemon
$1^1/_2$ tsp. Grenadine

Shake with ice and strain
into cocktail glass.

BOSTON COOLER

Into collins glass, put the
juice of $^1/_2$ lemon, 1 tsp.
powdered sugar, and 2 oz.
carbonated water. Stir.
Then fill glass with cracked
ice and add:
2 oz. Mr. Boston Rum

Fill with carbonated water
or ginger ale and stir again.
Add spiral of orange or
lemon peel (or both) and
dangle end over rim of
glass.

BOSTON GOLD

1 oz. Mr. Boston Vodka
$^1/_2$ oz. Mr. Boston
 Crème de Banana
 Orange Juice

Pour vodka and banana
liqueur over ice cubes in
highball glass. Fill with
orange juice and stir.

BOSTON SIDECAR

$^3/_4$ oz. Mr. Boston Five
 Star Brandy
$^3/_4$ oz. Mr. Boston Rum
$^3/_4$ oz. Mr. Boston Triple
 Sec
Juice of $^1/_2$ Lime

Shake with ice and strain
into cocktail glass.

BOSTON SOUR

Juice of $^1/_2$ Lemon
1 tsp. Powdered Sugar
2 oz. Old Thompson
 Blended Whiskey
1 Egg White

Shake with cracked ice and
strain into sour glass. Add a
slice of lemon and a
cherry.

BOURBON HIGHBALL

Fill highball glass with **2
oz. Kentucky Tavern
Bourbon**, ginger ale or
carbonated water, and ice
cubes. Add a twist of lemon
peel, if desired, and stir.

BRANDIED MADEIRA

1 oz. Mr. Boston Five
Star Brandy
1 oz. Madeira
$1/2$ oz. Dry Vermouth

Stir with cracked ice and
strain into old-fashioned
glass over ice cubes. Add a
twist of lemon peel.

BRANDIED PORT

1 oz. Mr. Boston Five
Star Brandy
1 oz. Tawny Port
1 tbsp. Lemon Juice
1 tsp. Maraschino

Shake all ingredients and
strain into old-fashioned
glass with ice cubes. Add a
slice of orange.

BRANDY ALEXANDER

$1/2$ oz. Mr. Boston
Crème de Cacao
(Brown)
$1/2$ oz. Mr. Boston Five
Star Brandy
$1/2$ oz. Heavy Cream

Shake well with cracked ice
and strain into a cocktail
glass.

BRANDY AND SODA

Pour 2 oz. Mr. Boston Five
Star Brandy into collins
glass with ice cubes. Add
carbonated water.

BRANDY BLAZER

1 lump Sugar
1 piece Orange Peel
2 oz. Mr. Boston Five
Star Brandy

Combine ingredients in
old-fashioned glass. Light
the liquid with match, stir
with long spoon for a few
seconds, and strain into hot
whiskey mug.

BRANDY CASSIS

$1^1/2$ oz. Mr. Boston Five
Star Brandy
1 oz. Lemon Juice
1 dash Mr. Boston
Crème de Cassis

Shake with cracked ice and
strain into cocktail glass.
Add a twist of lemon peel.

BRANDY COBBLER

1 tsp. Powdered Sugar
2 oz. Carbonated
Water
2 oz. Mr. Boston Five
Star Brandy

Dissolve powdered sugar in
carbonated water. Fill 10
oz. goblet with shaved ice.
Add brandy. Stir well and
decorate with fruits in
season. Serve with straws.

BRANDY COCKTAIL

2 oz. Mr. Boston Five
Star Brandy
$1/4$ tsp. Sugar Syrup
2 dashes Bitters

Stir with ice and strain into
cocktail glass. Add a twist of
lemon peel.

BRANDY COLLINS
Juice of $1/2$ Lemon
1 tsp. Powdered Sugar
2 oz. Mr. Boston Five
Star Brandy

Shake with cracked ice and strain into collins glass. Add cubes of ice, fill with carbonated water, and stir. Decorate with a slice of orange or lemon and a cherry. Serve with straws.

BRANDY CRUSTA COCKTAIL
Moisten the edge of a cocktail glass with lemon and dip into sugar. Cut the rind of half a lemon in a spiral and place in glass.

1 tsp. Maraschino
1 dash Bitters
1 tsp. Lemon Juice
$1/2$ oz. Mr. Boston Triple Sec
2 oz. Mr. Boston Five Star Brandy

Stir above ingredients with ice and strain into sugar-rimmed glass. Add a slice of orange.

BRANDY DAISY
Juice of $1/2$ Lemon
$1/2$ tsp. Powdered Sugar
1 tsp. Raspberry Syrup or Grenadine
2 oz. Mr. Boston Five Star Brandy

Shake with ice and strain into stein or 8 oz. metal cup. Add cubes of ice and decorate with fruit.

BRANDY EGGNOG
1 Whole Egg
1 tsp. Powdered Sugar
2 oz. Mr. Boston Five Star Brandy

Shake with ice and strain into collins glass. Fill glass with milk. Sprinkle nutmeg on top.

BRANDY FIX
Juice of $1/2$ Lemon
1 tsp. Powdered Sugar
1 tsp. Water
$2^1/2$ oz. Mr. Boston Five Star Brandy

Mix lemon juice, powdered sugar, and water in a highball glass. Stir. Then fill glass with shaved ice and brandy. Stir, add a slice of lemon. Serve with straws.

BRANDY FIZZ
Juice of $1/2$ Lemon
1 tsp. Powdered Sugar
2 oz. Mr. Boston Five Star Brandy

Shake with cracked ice and strain into highball glass over two ice cubes. Fill with carbonated water.

BRANDY FLIP
1 Whole Egg
1 tsp. Powdered Sugar
$1^1/2$ oz. Mr. Boston Five Star Brandy
2 tsps. Light Cream (if desired)

Shake with ice and strain into flip glass. Sprinkle a little nutmeg on top.

BRANDY GUMP COCKTAIL

1½ oz. Mr. Boston Five Star Brandy
Juice of ½ Lemon
½ tsp. Grenadine

Shake with ice and strain into cocktail glass.

BRANDY HIGHBALL

In a highball glass pour 2 oz. Mr. Boston Five Star Brandy, over ice cubes and fill with ginger ale or carbonated water. Add a twist of lemon peel, if desired, and stir gently.

BRANDY JULEP

Into collins glass put 1 tsp. powdered sugar, five or six leaves fresh mint, and 2½ oz. Mr. Boston Five Star Brandy. Then fill glass with finely shaved ice, and stir until mint rises to top, being careful not to bruise leaves. (Do not hold glass with hand while stirring.) Decorate with a slice of pineapple, orange, or lemon and a cherry. Serve with straws.

BRANDY MILK PUNCH

1 tsp. Powdered Sugar
2 oz. Mr. Boston Five Star Brandy
1 cup Milk

Shake with ice, strain into collins glass, and sprinkle nutmeg on top.

BRANDY PUNCH

Juice of 1 dozen Lemons
Juice of 4 Oranges

Add enough sugar to sweeten and mix with:

1 cup Grenadine
32 oz. Carbonated Water

Pour over large block of ice in punch bowl and stir well. Then add:

1 cup Mr. Boston Triple Sec
1.75 Liter Mr. Boston Five Star Brandy
2 cups Tea (optional)

Stir well and decorate with fruits in season. Serve in punch glasses.

BRANDY SANGAREE

Dissolve ½ tsp. powdered sugar in 1 tsp. of water, and add:

2 oz. Mr. Boston Five Star Brandy

Pour into highball glass over ice cubes. Fill with carbonated water. Stir. Float a tbsp. of port on top and sprinkle lightly with nutmeg.

BRANDY SLING 🥃

Dissolve 1 tsp. powdered sugar in tsp. of water and juice of $\frac{1}{2}$ lemon. Add:

 2 oz. Mr. Boston Five Star Brandy

Serve in old-fashioned cocktail glass with cubed ice and twist of lemon peel.

BRANDY SMASH 🥃

Muddle 1 lump sugar with 1 oz. carbonated water and 4 sprigs of fresh mint. Add:

 2 oz. Mr. Boston Five Star Brandy

and ice cubes. Stir and decorate with a slice of orange and a cherry. Add a twist of lemon peel on top. Use old-fashioned cocktail glass.

BRANDY SOUR

 Juice of $\frac{1}{2}$ Lemon
 $\frac{1}{2}$ tsp. Powdered Sugar
 2 oz. Mr. Boston Five Star Brandy

Shake with ice and strain into sour glass. Decorate with a half slice of lemon and a cherry.

BRANDY SQUIRT

 $1\frac{1}{2}$ oz. Mr. Boston Five Star Brandy
 1 tbsp. Powdered Sugar
 1 tsp. Grenadine

Shake with ice and strain into highball glass and fill with carbonated water. Decorate with stick of pineapple and strawberries.

BRANDY SWIZZLE

Made same as Gin Swizzle (see page 90) using

 2 oz. Mr. Boston Five Star Brandy.

BRANDY TODDY 🥃

In an old-fashioned glass dissolve:

 $\frac{1}{2}$ tsp. Powdered Sugar
 1 tsp. Water

Add:

 2 oz. Mr. Boston Five Star Brandy
 1 Ice Cube

Stir and add a twist of lemon peel on top.

BRANDY TODDY (HOT) 🥃

Put lump of sugar into hot whiskey glass and fill two-thirds with boiling water. Add:

 2 oz. Mr. Boston Five Star Brandy

Stir and decorate with a slice of lemon. Sprinkle nutmeg on top.

BRANDY VERMOUTH COCKTAIL

 $\frac{1}{2}$ oz. Sweet Vermouth
 2 oz. Mr. Boston Five Star Brandy
 1 dash Bitters

Stir with ice and strain into cocktail glass.

BRANTINI

1 1/2 oz. Mr. Boston Five Star Brandy
1 oz. Mr. Boston Gin
1 dash Dry Vermouth

Stir with cracked ice and strain into old-fashioned glass with cubed ice. Add a twist of lemon peel.

BRAVE BULL

1 1/2 oz. Gavilan Tequila
1 oz. Expresso® Coffee Liqueur

Pour over ice cubes in old-fashioned glass and stir. Add a twist of lemon.

BRAZIL COCKTAIL

1 1/2 oz. Dry Vermouth
1 1/2 oz. Dry Sherry
1 dash Bitters
1/4 tsp. Absinthe Substitute

Stir with ice and strain into cocktail glass.

BREAKFAST EGGNOG

1 Whole Egg
1/2 oz. Mr. Boston Triple Sec
2 oz. Mr. Boston Apricot Flavored Brandy
6 oz. Milk

Shake well with cracked ice and strain into collins glass. Sprinkle nutmeg on top.

BRIGHTON PUNCH

3/4 oz. Kentucky Tavern Bourbon
3/4 oz. Mr. Boston Five Star Brandy
3/4 oz. Benedictine
Juice of 1/2 Orange
Juice of 1/2 Lemon

Shake with ice and pour into collins glass nearly filled with shaved ice. Then fill with carbonated water and stir gently. Decorate with orange and lemon slices and serve with straw.

BROKEN SPUR COCKTAIL

3/4 oz. Sweet Vermouth
1 1/2 oz. Port
1/4 tsp. Mr. Boston Triple Sec

Stir with ice and strain into cocktail glass.

BRONX COCKTAIL

1 oz. Mr. Boston Gin
1/2 oz. Dry Vermouth
1/2 oz. Sweet Vermouth
Juice of 1/4 Orange

Shake with ice and strain into cocktail glass. Serve with slice of orange.

BRONX COCKTAIL (DRY)

1 oz. Mr. Boston Gin
1 oz. Dry Vermouth
Juice of 1/4 Orange

Shake with ice and strain into cocktail glass. Serve with slice of orange.

BRONX GOLDEN COCKTAIL

Same as Bronx Cocktail with the addition of one egg yolk. Use flip glass.

BRONX SILVER COCKTAIL

Juice of $1/2$ Orange
1 Egg White
$1/2$ oz.   Dry Vermouth
1 oz.   Mr. Boston Gin
Shake with ice and strain into flip glass.

BRONX TERRACE COCKTAIL

$1^1/_2$ oz. Mr. Boston Gin
$1^1/_2$ oz. Dry Vermouth
Juice of $1/2$ Lime
Shake with ice and strain into cocktail glass. Add a cherry.

BROWN COCKTAIL

$3/_4$ oz.   Mr. Boston Gin
$3/_4$ oz.   Mr. Boston Rum
$3/_4$ oz.   Dry Vermouth
Stir with ice and strain into cocktail glass.

BUCK JONES

$1^1/_2$ oz. Mr. Boston Rum
1 oz.   Sweet Sherry
Juice of $1/2$ Lime
Pour ingredients into highball glass over ice cubes and stir. Fill with ginger ale.

BUCKS FIZZ (MIMOSA)

Pour 2 oz. orange juice in a collins glass over two cubes of ice, fill with **Shadow Creek Champagne**, and stir very gently.

BULLDOG COCKTAIL

$1^1/_2$ oz. Mr. Boston Cherry Flavored Brandy
$3/_4$ oz.   Mr. Boston Gin
Juice of $1/2$ Lime
Shake with ice and strain into cocktail glass.

BULLDOG HIGHBALL

Juice of $1/2$ Orange
2 oz.   Mr. Boston Gin
Pour into highball glass over ice cubes and fill with ginger ale. Stir.

BULL FROG

$1^1/_2$ oz. Mr. Boston Vodka
5 oz.   Lemonade
Pour over ice in a tall glass and garnish with a slice of lime.

BULL SHOT

1½ oz. Mr. Boston Vodka
3 oz. Chilled Beef
Bouillon
1 dash Worcestershire
Sauce
1 dash Salt and Pepper
Shake with cracked ice and
strain into old-fashioned
glass.

BULL'S EYE

1 oz. Mr. Boston Five
Star Brandy
2 oz. Hard Cider
Pour into highball glass
over ice cubes and fill with
ginger ale. Stir.

BULL'S MILK

1 tsp. Powdered Sugar
1 oz. Mr. Boston Rum
1½ oz. Mr. Boston Five
Star Brandy
1 cup Milk
Shake with ice and strain
into collins glass. Sprinkle
nutmeg and pinch of
cinnamon on top.

BURGUNDY BISHOP

Juice of ¼ Lemon
1 tsp. Powdered Sugar
1 oz. Mr. Boston Rum
Shake with ice and strain
into highball glass over ice
cubes. Fill with Corbet
Canyon Vineyards
burgundy wine and stir.
Decorate with fruits.

BUSHRANGER

1½ oz. Mr. Boston Rum
1 oz. Dubonnet®
1 dash Bitters
Stir with cracked ice and
strain into cocktail glass.

BUTTON HOOK
COCKTAIL

½ oz. Mr. Boston
Crème de Menthe
(White)
½ oz. Mr. Boston
Apricot Flavored
Brandy
½ oz. Absinthe
Substitute
½ oz. Mr. Boston Five
Star Brandy
Shake with ice and strain
into cocktail glass.

C

CABARET

1½ oz. Mr. Boston Gin
2 dashes Bitters
½ tsp. Dry Vermouth
¼ tsp. Benedictine

Stir with ice and strain into cocktail glass. Serve with a cherry.

CABLEGRAM

Juice of ½ Lemon
1 tsp. Powdered Sugar
2 oz. Old Thompson Blended Whiskey

Stir with ice cubes in highball glass and fill with ginger ale.

CADIZ

¾ oz. Dry Sherry
¾ oz. Mr. Boston Blackberry Flavored Brandy
½ oz. Mr. Boston Triple Sec
1 tbsp. Light Cream

Shake with ice and strain into old-fashioned glass over ice cubes.

CAFÉ DE PARIS COCKTAIL

1 Egg White
1 tsp. Absinthe Substitute
1 tsp. Light Cream
1½ oz. Mr. Boston Gin

Shake with ice and strain into cocktail glass.

CAFÉ DI SARONNO

Add 1 oz. Amaretto di Saronno to a cup of black coffee. Top with whipped cream.

CAFÉ ROYALE

1 Sugar Cube
Mr. Boston Five Star Brandy
1 cup Hot Black Coffee

Put cube of sugar, well soaked with brandy, in teaspoon and hold so that it will rest on top of the cup of coffee and ignite. Hold until flame burns out. Drop contents in coffee.

CALEDONIA

1 oz.   Mr. Boston
        Brown Crème de
        Cacao
1 oz.   Mr. Boston Five
        Star Brandy
1 oz.   Milk
1 Egg Yolk

Shake well with ice and
strain into old-fashioned
glass over ice cubes.
Sprinkle cinnamon on top.

CALIFORNIA LEMONADE

Juice of 1 Lemon
Juice of 1 Lime
1 tbsp. Powdered Sugar
2 oz.   Old Thompson
        Blended Whiskey
1/4 tsp. Grenadine

Shake with ice and strain
into collins glass over
shaved ice. Fill with
carbonated water and
decorate with slices of
orange and lemon, and a
cherry. Serve with straws.

CALM VOYAGE

1/2 oz. Strega
1/2 oz. Mr. Boston Rum
1 tbsp. Passion Fruit
         Syrup
2 tsps. Lemon Juice
1/2 Egg White

Put all ingredients in
blender with half a cup of
crushed ice. Blend at low
speed and pour into
champagne glass.

CAMERON'S KICK COCKTAIL

3/4 oz. Desmond & Duff
         Scotch
3/4 oz. Irish Whisky
Juice of 1/4 Lemon
2 dashes Orange Bitters

Shake with ice and strain
into cocktail glass.

CANADIAN CHERRY

1 1/2 oz. Mr. Boston Five
          Star Canadian Whisky
1/2 oz.   Mr. Boston
          Cherry Flavored
          Brandy
1 1/2 tsps. Lemon Juice
1 1/2 tsps. Orange Juice

Shake all ingredients and
strain into old-fashioned
glass over ice cubes.
Moisten glass rim with
cherry brandy.

CANADIAN COCKTAIL

1 1/2 oz. Mr. Boston Five
          Star Canadian Whisky
1 dash Bitters
1 1/2 tsps. Mr. Boston
          Triple Sec
1 tsp.   Powdered Sugar

Shake with ice and strain
into cocktail glass.

CANADIAN PINEAPPLE

1 1/2 oz. Mr. Boston Five
          Star Canadian Whisky
1 tsp.   Pineapple Juice
1 tbsp.   Lemon Juice
1/2 tsp. Maraschino

Shake with ice and strain
into old-fashioned glass
over ice cubes. Add a stick
of pineapple.

Canadian Pineapple

CANADO SALUDO

1½ oz. Mr. Boston Rum
1 oz. Orange Juice
1 oz. Pineapple Juice
5 dashes Lemon Juice
5 dashes Grenadine
5 dashes Bitters

Serve in a 6 oz. glass with pineapple slices, orange slice, and a cherry over ice cubes.

CANAL STREET DAISY

Juice of ¼ Lemon
Juice of ¼ Orange
1 oz. Old Thompson Blended Whiskey

Pour all ingredients into a collins glass over ice cubes. Add carbonated water and an orange slice.

CAPE CODDER

1½ oz. Mr. Boston Vodka or Mr. Boston Rum
3 oz. Cranberry Juice
Juice of ½ Lime (if desired)

Serve on the rocks in old-fashioned glass or highball glass with carbonated water.

CAPPUCINO COCKTAIL

¾ oz. Mr. Boston Coffee Flavored Brandy
¾ oz. Mr. Boston Vodka
¾ oz. Light Cream

Shake well with ice. Strain into cocktail glass.

CAPRI

¾ oz. Mr. Boston Crème de Cacao (White)
¾ oz. Mr. Boston Crème de Banana
¾ oz. Light Cream

Shake with ice and strain into old-fashioned glass over ice cubes.

CARA SPOSA

1 oz. Mr. Boston Coffee Flavored Brandy
1 oz. Mr. Boston Triple Sec
½ oz. Light Cream

Shake with ice and strain into cocktail glass.

CARDINAL PUNCH

Juice of 1 dozen Lemons
Add enough powdered sugar to sweeten. Pour over large block of ice in punch bowl and stir well. Then add:

16 oz. Mr. Boston Five Star Brandy
16 oz. Mr. Boston Rum
1 split Shadow Creek Champagne
64 oz. Claret
32 oz. Carbonated Water
8 oz. Sweet Vermouth
16 oz. Strong Tea (optional)

Stir well and decorate with fruits in season. Serve in punch glasses.

CARIBBEAN CHAMPAGNE

1/2 tsp. Mr. Boston Rum
1/2 tsp. Mr. Boston
         Crème de Banana
         Chilled Shadow Creek
         Champagne

Pour rum and banana liqueur into champagne glass. Fill with champagne and stir lightly. Add a slice of banana.

CARROL COCKTAIL

1 1/2 oz. Mr. Boston Five
          Star Brandy
3/4 oz.   Sweet Vermouth

Stir with ice and strain into cocktail glass. Serve with a cherry.

CARUSO

1 1/2 oz. Mr. Boston Gin
1 oz.   Dry Vermouth
1/2 oz.   Mr. Boston
          Crème de Menthe
          (Green)

Stir with ice and strain into cocktail glass.

CASA BLANCA

2 oz.   Mr. Boston Rum
1 1/2 tsps. Lime Juice
1 1/2 tsps. Mr. Boston
           Triple Sec
1 1/2 tsps. Maraschino

Shake with ice and strain into cocktail glass.

CASINO COCKTAIL

2 dashes Orange Bitters
1/4 tsp. Maraschino
1/4 tsp. Lemon Juice
2 oz.   Mr. Boston Dry
         Gin

Shake with ice and strain into cocktail glass. Serve with a cherry.

CHAMPAGNE COCKTAIL

1 lump   Sugar
2 dashes Bitters

Place in champagne glass and fill with Shadow Creek champagne. Add a twist of lemon peel.

CHAMPAGNE CUP

4 tsps. Powdered Sugar
6 oz.   Carbonated
        Water
1 oz.   Mr. Boston Triple
        Sec
2 oz.   Mr. Boston Five
        Star Brandy

Fill large glass pitcher with cubes of ice and ingredients above. Add 16 oz. chilled Shadow Creek champagne. Stir well and decorate with seasonal fruits and also rind of cucumber inserted on each side of pitcher. Top with a small bunch of mint. Serve in wine glasses.

CHAMPAGNE PUNCH ♥

Juice of 1 dozen Lemons
Add enough powdered
sugar to sweeten. Pour over
large block of ice in punch
bowl and stir well. Then
add:

- 1 cup   Maraschino
- 1 cup   Mr. Boston Triple Sec
- 16 oz.   Mr. Boston Five Star Brandy
- 2 750ml bottles Shadow Creek Champagne
- 16 oz.   Carbonated Water
- 16 oz.   Strong Tea (optional)

Stir well and decorate with
fruits in season. Serve in
punch glasses.

CHAMPAGNE SHERBET PUNCH

- ♥ 2 750ml bottles Shadow Creek Champagne
- 1 750ml bottle Sauterne
- 32 oz.   Lemon or Pineapple Sherbert

Put sherbet in punch bowl.
Add sauterne and
champagne. Decorate with
lemon slices or pineapple
chunks.

CHAMPAGNE VELVET

See Black Velvet recipe on
page 42.

CHAMPS ÉLYSÉES COCKTAIL

- 1 oz.   Mr. Boston Five Star Brandy
- 1/2 oz.   Chartreuse (Yellow)
- Juice of 1/4 Lemon
- 1/2 tsp.   Powdered Sugar
- 1 dash   Bitters

Shake with ice and strain
into cocktail glass.

CHAPALA

- 1 1/2 oz.   Gavilan Tequila
- 1 tbsp.   Orange Juice
- 1 tbsp.   Lemon Juice
- 1 dash   Mr. Boston Triple Sec
- 2 tsps.   Grenadine

Shake with ice and strain
into old-fashioned glass
over ice cubes. Add a slice
of orange.

CHAPEL HILL

- 1 1/2 oz.   Kentucky Tavern Bourbon
- 1/2 oz.   Mr. Boston Triple Sec
- 1 tbsp.   Lemon Juice

Shake with ice and strain
into cocktail glass. Add
twist of orange peel.

CHARLES COCKTAIL

- 1 1/2 oz.   Sweet Vermouth
- 1 1/2 oz.   Mr. Boston Five Star Brandy
- 1 dash   Bitters

Stir with ice and strain into
cocktail glass.

CHARLIE CHAPLIN

1 oz.   Mr. Boston Sloe
        Gin
1 oz.   Mr. Boston
        Apricot Flavored
        Brandy
1 oz.   Lemon Juice

Shake with ice and strain
into old-fashioned glass
over ice cubes.

CHATEAU BRIAND'S RUM COW*

1 oz.   Mr. Boston Dark
          Rum
$1/4$ oz. Meyer's Rum
1 tsp.   Sugar
2 dashes Bitters
$3/4$ cup milk

Blend and strain into a
collins glass.

CHELSEA SIDECAR

Juice of $1/4$ Lemon
$3/4$ oz. Mr. Boston Triple
          Sec
$3/4$ oz. Mr. Boston Gin

Shake with ice and strain
into cocktail glass.

CHERIE

Juice of 1 Lime
$1/2$ oz. Mr. Boston Triple
          Sec
1 oz.   Mr. Boston Rum
$1/2$ oz. Mr. Boston
          Cherry Flavored
          Brandy

Shake with ice and strain
into cocktail glass. Add a
cherry.

CHERRY BLOSSOM

$1^1/2$ oz. Mr. Boston Five
           Star Brandy
$1/2$ oz.   Mr. Boston
           Cherry Flavored
           Brandy
$1^1/2$ tsps. Mr. Boston
           Triple Sec
$1^1/2$ tsps. Grenadine
2 tsps.   Lemon Juice

Shake with ice and strain
into cocktail glass which
has had its rim moistened
with cherry brandy and
dipped into powdered
sugar. Add a maraschino
cherry.

CHERRY COOLER

2 oz.   Mr. Boston
        Cherry Vodka
        Cola

Pour cherry vodka into
collins glass over ice cubes.
Fill with cola, add a slice of
lemon, and stir.

CHERRY FIZZ

Juice of $1/2$ Lemon
2 oz.   Mr. Boston
        Cherry Flavored
        Brandy

Shake with ice and strain
into highball glass with two
ice cubes. Fill with
carbonated water and
decorate with a cherry.

*Chateau Briand,
Dallas, Texas

CHERRY FLIP

1 Whole Egg
1 tsp. Powdered Sugar
1½ oz. Mr. Boston
    Cherry Flavored
    Brandy
2 tsps. Light Cream (if
    desired)

Shake with ice and strain into flip glass. Sprinkle a little nutmeg on top.

CHERRY RUM

1¼ oz. Mr. Boston Rum
1½ tsps. Mr. Boston
    Cherry Flavored
    Brandy
1 tbsp. Light Cream

Shake with ice and strain into cocktail glass.

CHERRY SLING

2 oz. Mr. Boston
    Cherry Flavored
    Brandy
Juice of ½ Lemon

Serve in old-fashioned glass with ice cubes and stir. Add a twist of lemon peel.

CHERRY WINE COCKTAIL

¾ oz. Danish Cherry
    Wine
¾ oz. Mr. Boston Vodka
Juice of ½ Lime

Shake with ice and strain into cocktail glass.

CHICAGO COCKTAIL

2 oz. Mr. Boston Five
    Star Brandy
1 dash Bitters
¼ tsp. Mr. Boston Triple
    Sec

Prepare old-fashioned glass by rubbing slice of lemon around rim and then dip in powdered sugar. Stir ingredients above with ice and strain into prepared glass.

CHICAGO FIZZ

Juice of ½ Lemon
1 tsp. Powdered Sugar
1 Egg White
1 oz. Port
1 oz. Mr. Boston Rum

Shake with ice and strain into highball glass over two ice cubes. Fill with carbonated water and stir.

CHINESE COCKTAIL

1 tbsp. Grenadine
1½ oz. Jamaica Rum
1 dash Bitters
1 tsp. Maraschino
1 tsp. Mr. Boston Triple
    Sec

Shake with ice and strain into cocktail glass.

CHOCOLATE COCKTAIL

1½ oz. Port
1½ tsps. Chartreuse
    (Yellow)
1 Egg Yolk
1 tsp. Powdered Sugar

Shake with ice and strain into flip glass.

CHOCOLATE DAISY
Juice of $1/2$ Lemon
$1/2$ tsp. Powdered Sugar
1 tsp. Grenadine
$1^1/2$ oz. Mr. Boston Five
Star Brandy
$1^1/2$ oz. Port
Shake with ice and strain
into stein or metal cup.
Add ice cubes and decorate
with fruit.

CHOCOLATE FLIP
1 Whole Egg
1 tsp. Powdered Sugar
$3/4$ oz. Mr. Boston Sloe
Gin
$3/4$ oz. Mr. Boston Five
Star Brandy
2 tsps. Light Cream (if
desired)
Shake with ice and strain
into flip glass. Sprinkle a
little nutmeg on top.

CHOCOLATE RUM
1 oz. Mr. Boston Rum
$1/2$ oz. Mr. Boston
Crème de Cacao
(Brown)
$1/2$ oz. Mr. Boston
Crème de Menthe
(White)
1 tbsp. Light Cream
1 tsp. 151 Proof Rum
Shake with ice and strain
into old-fashioned glass
over ice cubes.

CHOCOLATE SOLDIER
Juice of $1/2$ Lime
$3/4$ oz. Dubonnet®
$1^1/2$ oz. Mr. Boston Gin
Shake with ice and strain
into cocktail glass.

CHRISTMAS YULE
EGGNOG
Beat first the yolks and
then, in a separate bowl,
the whites of 1 dozen eggs.
Pour them together and
add:
1 pinch Baking Soda
6 oz. Mr. Boston Rum
2 lbs. Granulated Sugar
Beat into stiff batter. Then
add:
32 oz. Milk
32 oz. Light Cream
1.75 Liter Old Thompson
Blended Whiskey
Stir. Set in refrigerator
overnight. Before serving,
stir again, and serve in
punch glasses. Sprinkle
nutmeg on top.

CIDER CUP
4 tsps. Powdered Sugar
6 oz. Carbonated
Water
1 oz. Mr. Boston Triple
Sec
2 oz. Mr. Boston Five
Star Brandy
16 oz. Apple Cider
Fill large glass pitcher with
ice. Stir in the ingredients
and decorate with as many
fruits as available and a
rind of cucumber inserted
on each side of pitcher.
Top with a small bunch of
mint. Serve in claret
glasses.

CIDER EGGNOG

1 Whole Egg
1 tsp.   Powdered Sugar
$^1/_2$ cup Milk

Shake with ice and strain into collins glass. Then fill the glass with cider and stir. Sprinkle nutmeg on top.

CLAMATO COCKTAIL

1$^1/_2$ oz. Mr. Boston Vodka
1 oz.   Clam Juice
3 oz.   Tomato Juice

Shake with ice, strain, and serve over ice cubes in old-fashioned glass.

CLARET COBBLER

1 tsp.   Powdered Sugar
2 oz.   Carbonated
         Water
3 oz.   Claret

Dissolve powdered sugar in carbonated water and then add claret. Fill goblet with ice and stir. Decorate with fruits in season. Serve with straws.

CLARET CUP

4 tsps. Powdered Sugar
6 oz.   Carbonated
         Water
1 oz.   Mr. Boston Triple
         Sec
2 oz.   Mr. Boston Five
         Star Brandy
16 oz.   Claret

Fill large glass pitcher with ice. Stir in the ingredients and decorate with as many fruits as available and a rind of cucumber inserted on each side of pitcher. Top with a small bunch of mint. Serve in claret glass.

CLARET PUNCH

Juice of 1 dozen
     Lemons

Add enough powdered sugar to sweeten. Pour over large block of ice in punch bowl and stir well. Then add:

1 cup Mr. Boston Triple
      Sec
16 oz.   Mr. Boston Five
         Star Brandy
3 750ml bottles Claret
32 oz.   Carbonated
         Water
32 oz.   Strong Tea
         (optional)

Stir and decorate with fruits in season. Serve in punch glasses.

Bourbon straight-up and on-the-rocks

CLARIDGE COCKTAIL

- $^3/_4$ oz. Mr. Boston Gin
- $^3/_4$ oz. Dry Vermouth
- 1 tbsp. Mr. Boston Apricot Flavored Brandy
- 1 tbsp. Mr. Boston Triple Sec

Stir with ice and strain into cocktail glass.

CLASSIC COCKTAIL

- Juice of $^1/_4$ Lemon
- $1^1/_2$ tsps. Curaçao
- $1^1/_2$ tsps. Maraschino
- 1 oz. Mr. Boston Five Star Brandy

Prepare rim of old-fashioned glass by rubbing with lemon and dipping into powdered sugar. Shake ingredients with ice and strain into prepared glass.

CLOVE COCKTAIL

- 1 oz. Sweet Vermouth
- $^1/_2$ oz. Mr. Boston Sloe Gin
- $^1/_2$ oz. Muscatel

Stir with ice and strain into cocktail glass.

CLOVER CLUB COCKTAIL

- Juice of $^1/_2$ Lemon
- 2 tsps. Grenadine
- 1 Egg White
- $1^1/_2$ oz. Mr. Boston Gin

Shake with ice and strain into cocktail glass.

CLOVER LEAF COCKTAIL

- Juice of 1 Lime
- 2 tsps. Grenadine
- 1 Egg White
- $1^1/_2$ oz. Mr. Boston Gin

Shake with ice and strain into cocktail glass. Serve with mint leaf on top.

CLUB COCKTAIL

- $1^1/_2$ oz. Mr. Boston Gin
- $^3/_4$ oz. Sweet Vermouth

Stir with ice and strain into cocktail glass. Add a cherry or olive.

COBBLERS

See Index on page 257 for complete list of Cobbler recipes.

COCOMACOQUE

- Juice of $^1/_2$ Lemon
- 2 oz. Pineapple Juice
- 2 oz. Orange Juice
- $1^1/_2$ oz. Mr. Boston Rum
- 2 oz. Valley Ridge Burgundy

Shake all ingredients except wine. Pour into collins glass over ice cubes and top with wine. Add pineapple stick.

COFFEE COCKTAIL

- 1 Whole Egg
- 1 tsp. Powdered Sugar
- 1 oz. Port
- 1 oz. Mr. Boston Five Star Brandy

Shake with ice and strain into flip glass. Sprinkle nutmeg on top.

COFFEE FLIP
1 Whole Egg
1 tsp. Powdered Sugar
1 oz. Mr. Boston Five
    Star Brandy
1 oz. Port
2 tsps. Light Cream (if
    desired)

Shake with ice and strain
into flip glass. Sprinkle a
little nutmeg on top.

COFFEE GRASSHOPPER
3/4 oz. Mr. Boston
    Coffee Flavored Brandy
3/4 oz. Mr. Boston
    Crème de Menthe
    (White)
3/4 oz. Light Cream

Shake with ice and strain
into old-fashioned glass
over ice cubes.

COFFEE SOUR
1 1/2 oz. Mr. Boston
    Coffee Flavored Brandy
1 oz. Lemon Juice
1 tsp. Powdered Sugar
1/2 Egg White

Shake with ice and strain
into sour glass.

COGNAC COUPLING
2 oz. Cognac
1 oz. Tawny Port
1/2 oz. Absinthe
    Substitute
1 tsp. Lemon Juice

Shake with ice and strain
into old-fashioned glass
over ice cubes.

COGNAC HIGHBALL
2 oz. Cognac
Ginger Ale or Carbonated
    Water

Pour cognac into highball
glass over ice cubes and fill
with ginger ale or
carbonated water. Add a
twist of lemon peel, if
desired, and stir.

COLD DECK COCKTAIL
1/2 tsp. Mr. Boston
    Crème de Menthe
    (White)
1/2 oz. Sweet Vermouth
1 oz. Mr. Boston Five
    Star Brandy

Stir with ice and strain into
cocktail glass.

COLE'S RASPBERRY
CREAM*
1 1/2 tbsps. Raspberry
    Yogurt
1 1/2 tbsps Raspberry Ice
    Cream
1 1/2 oz. Mr. Boston
    Crème de Cacao
    (White)
1 1/2 oz. Mr. Boston Vodka
2 oz. Heavy Cream

Shake or blend.

COLLINS
See Index on page 257 for
complete list of Collins
recipes.

*Cole's Restaurant,
Buffalo, NY

COLONIAL COCKTAIL
$^1/_2$ oz. Grapefruit Juice
1 tsp. Maraschino
$1^1/_2$ oz. Mr. Boston Gin
Shake with ice and strain into cocktail glass. Serve with an olive.

COMBO
$2^1/_2$ oz. Dry Vermouth
1 tsp. Mr. Boston Five Star Brandy
$^1/_2$ tsp. Mr. Boston Triple Sec
$^1/_2$ tsp. Powdered Sugar
1 dash Bitters
Shake with ice and strain into old-fashioned glass over ice cubes.

COMMODORE COCKTAIL
Juice of $^1/_2$ Lime or $^1/_4$ Lemon
1 tsp. Powdered Sugar
2 dashes Orange Bitters
$1^1/_2$ oz. Old Thompson Blended Whiskey
Shake with ice and strain into cocktail glass.

CONTINENTAL
$1^3/_4$ oz. Mr. Boston Rum
1 tbsp. Lime Juice
$1^1/_2$ tsps. Mr. Boston Crème de Menthe (Green)
$^1/_2$ tsp. Powdered Sugar
Shake with ice and strain into cocktail glass. Add a twist of lemon peel.

COOLERS
See Index on page 257 for complete list of Cooler recipes.

COOPERSTOWN COCKTAIL
$^1/_2$ oz. Dry Vermouth
$^1/_2$ oz. Sweet Vermouth
1 oz. Mr. Boston Gin
Shake with ice and strain into cocktail glass. Add a sprig of mint.

CORKSCREW
$1^1/_2$ oz. Mr. Boston Rum
$^1/_2$ oz. Dry Vermouth
$^1/_2$ oz. Mr. Boston Peach Flavored Brandy
Shake with ice and strain into cocktail glass. Garnish with a lime slice.

CORNELL COCKTAIL
$^1/_2$ tsp. Lemon Juice
1 tsp Maraschino
1 Egg White
$1^1/_2$ oz. Mr. Boston Gin
Shake with ice and strain into cocktail glass.

CORONATION COCKTAIL
$^3/_4$ oz. Mr. Boston Gin
$^3/_4$ oz. Dubonnet®
$^3/_4$ oz. Dry Vermouth
Stir with ice and strain into cocktail glass.

COUNT CURREY
- 1 1/2 oz. Mr. Boston Gin
- 1 tsp. Powdered Sugar
- Chilled Shadow Creek
  Champagne

Shake with ice and strain into champagne glass over ice cubes.

COUNTRY CLUB COOLER
- 1/2 tsp. Grenadine
- 2 oz. Carbonated Water
- 2 oz. Dry Vermouth

Into collins glass, put grenadine and carbonated water and stir. Add ice cubes and dry vermouth. Fill with carbonated water or ginger ale and stir again. Insert a spiral of orange or lemon peel (or both) and dangle end over rim of glass.

COWBOY COCKTAIL
- 1 1/2 oz. Old Thompson Blended Whiskey
- 1 tbsp. Light Cream

Shake with ice and strain into cocktail glass.

CREAM FIZZ
- Juice of 1/2 Lemon
- 1 tsp. Powdered Sugar
- 2 oz. Mr. Boston Gin
- 1 tsp. Light Cream

Shake with ice and strain into highball glass over two ice cubes. Fill with carbonated water and stir.

CREAM PUFF
- 2 oz. Mr. Boston Rum
- 1 oz. Light Cream
- 1/2 tsp. Powdered Sugar

Shake with ice and strain into highball glass over two ice cubes. Fill with carbonated water and stir.

CREAMSICLE
- 1 1/2 oz. Vanilla Liqueur
- 1 1/2 oz. Milk
- 3 oz. Orange Juice

Fill a tall glass with ice, add the above ingredients and stir.

CREAMY ORANGE
- 1 oz. Orange Juice
- 1 oz. Balfour Cream Sherry
- 3/4 oz. Mr. Boston Five Star Brandy
- 1 tbsp. Light Cream

Shake with ice and strain into cocktail glass.

CREAMY SCREWDRIVER
- 2 oz. Mr. Boston Vodka
- 1 Egg Yolk
- 6 oz. Orange Juice
- 1 tsp. Sugar

Combine all ingredients with a half-cup of crushed ice in an electric blender. Blend at low speed and pour into collins glass.

CRÈME DE CAFÉ

1 oz.   Mr. Boston
         Coffee Flavored Brandy
1/2 oz. Mr. Boston Rum
1/2 oz. Mr. Boston
         Anisette
1 oz.   Light Cream
Shake with ice and strain
into old-fashioned glass.

CRÈME DE GIN COCKTAIL

1 1/2 oz. Mr. Boston Gin
1/2 oz.   Mr. Boston
           Crème de Menthe
           (White)
1 Egg White
2 tsps.   Lemon Juice
2 tsps.   Orange Juice
Shake with ice and strain
into cocktail glass.

CRÈME DE MENTHE FRAPPÉ

Fill cocktail glass up to
brim with shaved ice. Add
Mr. Boston Crème de
Menthe (Green). Serve
with two short straws.

CREOLE

1 1/2 oz. Mr. Boston Rum
1 dash   Tobasco Sauce
1 tsp.   Lemon Juice
Salt and Pepper
Beef Bouillon
Shake with ice and strain
into old-fashioned glass
over ice cubes.

CREOLE LADY

1 1/2 oz. Kentucky Tavern
           Bourbon
1 1/2 oz. Madeira
1 tsp.   Grenadine
Stir with ice and strain into
cocktail glass. Serve with
one green and one red
cherry.

CRIMSON COCKTAIL

1 1/2 oz. Mr. Boston Gin
2 tsps.   Lemon Juice
1 tsp.   Grenadine
3/4 oz.   Port
Shake with ice and strain
into cocktail glass, leaving
enough room on top to
float port.

CRYSTAL SLIPPER COCKTAIL

1/2 oz.   Blue Curaçao
2 dashes Orange Bitters
1 1/2 oz. Mr. Boston Gin
Stir with ice and strain into
cocktail glass.

CUBA LIBRE

Juice of 1/2 Lime
2 oz.   Mr. Boston Rum
Cola
Put lime juice and rind in
glass, and add rum. Fill
highball glass with cola and
ice cubes.

CUBAN COCKTAIL NO. 1

Juice of 1/2 Lime
1/2 tsp.   Powdered Sugar
2 oz.   Mr. Boston Rum
Shake with ice and strain
into cocktail glass.

CUBAN COCKTAIL NO. 2
Juice of ¹/₂ Lime or ¹/₄
   Lemon
   ¹/₂ oz.   Mr. Boston
      Apricot Flavored
      Brandy
   1¹/₂ oz. Mr. Boston Five
      Star Brandy
   1 tsp.   Mr. Boston Rum
Shake with ice and strain
into cocktail glass.

CUBAN SPECIAL
1 tbsp. Pineapple Juice
Juice of ¹/₂ Lime
   1 oz.   Mr. Boston Rum
   ¹/₂ tsp. Mr. Boston Triple
      Sec
Shake with ice and strain
into cocktail glass. Decorate
with a slice of pineapple
and a cherry.

CUPS
See Index on page 258 for
complete list of Cup
recipes.

D

DAIQUIRI

Juice of 1 Lime
1 tsp. Powdered Sugar
1 1/2 oz. Mr. Boston Rum

Shake with ice and strain into cocktail glass.

DAISIES

Index on page 259 for complete list of Daisy recipes.

DAMN-THE-WEATHER COCKTAIL

1 tsp. Mr. Boston Triple Sec
1 tbsp. Orange Juice
1 tbsp. Sweet Vermouth
1 oz. Mr. Boston Gin

Shake with ice and strain into cocktail glass.

DARB COCKTAIL

1 tsp. Lemon Juice
3/4 oz. Dry Vermouth
3/4 oz. Mr. Boston Gin
3/4 oz. Mr. Boston Apricot Flavored Brandy

Shake with ice and strain into cocktail glass.

DEAUVILLE COCKTAIL

Juice of 1/4 Lemon
1/2 oz. Mr. Boston Five Star Brandy
1/2 oz. Mr. Boston Apple Brandy
1/2 oz. Mr. Boston Triple Sec

Shake with ice and strain into cocktail glass.

DEEP SEA COCKTAIL

1 oz. Dry Vermouth
1/4 tsp. Absinthe Substitute
1 dash Orange Bitters
1 oz. Mr. Boston Gin

Stir with ice and strain into cocktail glass.

DELMONICO NO. 1

3/4 oz. Mr. Boston Gin
1/2 oz. Dry Vermouth
1/2 oz. Sweet Vermouth
1/2 oz. Mr. Boston Five Star Brandy

Stir with ice and strain into cocktail glass. Add a twist of lemon peel.

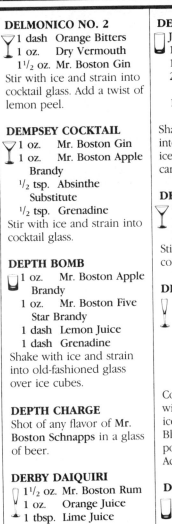

DELMONICO NO. 2

1 dash Orange Bitters
1 oz. Dry Vermouth
1½ oz. Mr. Boston Gin

Stir with ice and strain into cocktail glass. Add a twist of lemon peel.

DEMPSEY COCKTAIL

1 oz. Mr. Boston Gin
1 oz. Mr. Boston Apple Brandy
½ tsp. Absinthe Substitute
½ tsp. Grenadine

Stir with ice and strain into cocktail glass.

DEPTH BOMB

1 oz. Mr. Boston Apple Brandy
1 oz. Mr. Boston Five Star Brandy
1 dash Lemon Juice
1 dash Grenadine

Shake with ice and strain into old-fashioned glass over ice cubes.

DEPTH CHARGE

Shot of any flavor of **Mr. Boston Schnapps** in a glass of beer.

DERBY DAIQUIRI

1½ oz. Mr. Boston Rum
1 oz. Orange Juice
1 tbsp. Lime Juice
1 tsp. Sugar

Combine all ingredients with a half-cup of shaved ice in an electric blender. Blend at low speed. Pour into champagne glass.

DERBY FIZZ

Juice of ½ Lemon
1 tsp. Powdered Sugar
1 Whole Egg
2 oz. Desmond & Duff Scotch
1 tsp. Mr. Boston Triple Sec

Shake with ice and strain into highball glass over two ice cubes. Fill with carbonated water and stir.

DEVIL'S COCKTAIL

½ tsp. Lemon Juice
1½ oz. Port
1½ oz. Dry Vermouth

Stir with ice and strain into cocktail glass.

DEVIL'S TAIL

1½ oz. Mr. Boston Rum
1 oz. Mr. Boston Vodka
1 tbsp. Lime Juice
1½ tsp. Grenadine
1½ tsp. Mr. Boston Apricot Flavored Brandy

Combine all ingredients with a half-cup of crushed ice in an electric blender. Blend at low speed and pour into champagne glass. Add a twist of lime peel.

DIAMOND FIZZ

Juice of ½ Lemon
1 tsp. Powdered Sugar
2 oz. Mr. Boston Gin

Shake with ice and strain into highball glass over two cubes of ice. Fill with Shadow Creek champagne and stir.

Brandy straight-up and on-the-rocks

DIANA COCKTAIL
Mr. Boston Crème de
Menthe (White)
Mr. Boston Five Star
Brandy

Fill cocktail glass with ice,
then fill ³/₄ full with crème
de menthe and float brandy
on top.

DILLATINI COCKTAIL
See Special Martini Section
on pages 204 and 206.

DINAH COCKTAIL
Juice of ¹/₄ Lemon
¹/₂ tsp. Powdered Sugar
1¹/₂ oz. Old Thompson
Blended Whiskey

Shake well with ice and
strain into cocktail glass.
Serve with a mint leaf.

DIPLOMAT
1¹/₂ oz. Dry Vermouth
¹/₂ oz. Sweet Vermouth
2 dashes Bitters
¹/₂ tsp. Maraschino

Stir with ice and strain into
cocktail glass. Serve with a
half slice of lemon and a
cherry.

DIXIE COCKTAIL
Juice of ¹/₄ Orange
1 tbsp. Absinthe
Substitute
¹/₂ oz. Dry Vermouth
1 oz. Mr. Boston Gin

Shake with ice and strain
into cocktail glass.

DIXIE JULEP
Into a collins glass put:
1 tsp. Powdered Sugar
2¹/₂ oz. Kentucky Tavern
Bourbon

Fill with ice and stir gently
until glass is frosted.
Decorate with sprigs of
mint. Serve with straws.

DIXIE WHISKEY COCKTAIL
¹/₂ tsp. Powdered Sugar
1 dash Bitters
¹/₄ tsp. Mr. Boston Triple
Sec
¹/₂ tsp. Mr. Boston
Crème de Menthe
(White)
2 oz. Kentucky Tavern
Bourbon

Shake with ice and strain
into cocktail glass.

DR. COOK
³/₄ oz. Mr. Boston Gin
1 tbsp. Lemon Juice
1 dash Maraschino
1 Egg White

Shake with ice and strain
into wine glass.

DOUBLE STANDARD SOUR
Juice of ¹/₂ Lemon or 1
Lime
¹/₂ tsp. Powdered Sugar
³/₄ oz. Old Thompson
Blended Whiskey
³/₄ oz. Mr. Boston Gin
¹/₂ tsp. Grenadine

Shake with ice and strain
into sour glass. Decorate
with a half-slice of lemon
and a cherry.

DREAM COCKTAIL

- 3/4 oz. Mr. Boston Triple Sec
- 1 1/2 oz. Mr. Boston Five Star Brandy
- 1/4 tsp. Mr. Boston Anisette

Shake with ice and strain into cocktail glass.

DRY MARTINI

See Special Martini Section on pages 204 and 206.

DU BARRY COCKTAIL

- 1 dash Bitters
- 3/4 oz. Dry Vermouth
- 1/2 tsp. Absinthe Substitute
- 1 1/2 oz. Mr. Boston Gin

Stir with ice and strain into cocktail glass. Add a slice of orange.

DUBONNET® COCKTAIL

- 1 1/2 oz. Dubonnet®
- 3/4 oz. Mr. Boston Gin
- 1 dash Orange Bitters (if desired)

Stir with ice and strain into cocktail glass. Add a twist of lemon peel.

DUBONNET® FIZZ

- Juice of 1/2 Orange
- Juice of 1/4 Lemon
- 1 tsp. Mr. Boston Cherry Flavored Brandy
- 2 oz. Dubonnet®

Shake with ice and strain into highball glass over two ice cubes. Fill with carbonated water and stir.

DUBONNET® HIGHBALL

Put 2 oz. Dubonnet® in highball glass with two ice cubes and fill with ginger ale or carbonated water. Add a twist of lemon peel, if desired, and stir.

DUCHESS

- 1 1/2 oz. Absinthe Substitute
- 1/2 oz. Dry Vermouth
- 1/2 oz. Sweet Vermouth

Shake with ice and strain into cocktail glass.

DUKE COCKTAIL

- 1/2 oz. Mr. Boston Triple Sec
- 1 tsp. Orange Juice
- 2 tsp. Lemon Juice
- 1/2 tsp. Maraschino
- 1 Whole Egg

Shadowcreek Champagne to top

Add first five ingredients, shake with ice and strain into champagne glass. Fill with champagne and stir.

E

EAST INDIA COCKTAIL NO. 1
1½ oz. Mr. Boston Five Star Brandy
½ tsp. Pineapple Juice
½ tsp. Mr. Boston Triple Sec
1 tsp. Jamaica Rum
1 dash Bitters
Shake with ice and strain into cocktail glass. Add a twist of lemon peel and a cherry.

EAST INDIA COCKTAIL NO. 2
1½ oz. Dry Vermouth
1½ oz. Dry Sherry
1 dash Orange Bitters
Stir with ice and strain into cocktail glass.

ECLIPSE COCKTAIL
Grenadine
1 oz. Mr. Boston Gin
2 oz. Mr. Boston Sloe Gin
½ tsp. Lemon Juice
Put enough grenadine into cocktail glass to cover a ripe olive. Mix the above ingredients in ice and pour onto the grenadine so that they do not mix.

EGG SOUR
1 Whole Egg
1 tsp. Powdered Sugar
Juice of ½ Lemon
2 oz. Mr. Boston Five Star Brandy
¼ tsp. Mr. Boston Triple Sec
Shake with ice and strain into old-fashioned glass.

EGGNOGS
See Index on page 259 for complete list of Eggnog recipes.

ELK'S OWN COCKTAIL
1 Egg White
1½ oz. Old Thompson Blended Whiskey
¾ oz. Port
Juice of ¼ Lemon
1 tsp. Powdered Sugar
Shake with ice and strain into cocktail glass. Add a strip of pineapple.

EL PRESIDENTE COCKTAIL NO. 1

Juice of 1 Lime
1 tsp. Pineapple Juice
1 tsp. Grenadine
1 1/2 oz. Mr. Boston Rum

Shake with ice and strain into cocktail glass.

EL PRESIDENTE COCKTAIL NO. 2

3/4 oz. Dry Vermouth
1 1/2 oz. Mr. Boston Rum
1 dash Bitters

Stir with ice and strain into cocktail glass.

EMERALD ISLE COCKTAIL

2 oz. Mr. Boston Gin
1 tsp. Mr. Boston Crème de Menthe (Green)
3 dashes Bitters

Stir with ice and strain into cocktail glass.

EMERSON

1 1/2 oz. Mr. Boston Gin
1 oz. Sweet Vermouth
Juice of 1/2 Lime
1 tsp. Maraschino

Shake with ice and strain into cocktail glass.

ENGLISH HIGHBALL

3/4 oz. Mr. Boston Gin
3/4 oz. Mr. Boston Five Star Brandy
3/4 oz. Sweet Vermouth

Pour into highball glass over ice cubes and fill with ginger ale or carbonated water. Add a twist of lemon peel, if desired, and stir.

ENGLISH ROSE COCKTAIL

1 1/2 oz. Mr. Boston Gin
3/4 oz. Mr. Boston Apricot Flavored Brandy
3/4 oz. Dry Vermouth
1 tsp. Grenadine
1/4 tsp. Lemon Juice

Prepare rim of glass by rubbing with lemon and dipping in sugar. Shake all ingredients with ice and strain into cocktail glass. Serve with a cherry.

ETHEL DUFFY COCKTAIL

3/4 oz. Mr. Boston Apricot Flavored Brandy
3/4 oz. Mr. Boston Crème de Menthe (White)
3/4 oz. Mr. Boston Triple Sec

Shake with ice and strain into cocktail glass.

EVERYBODY'S IRISH COCKTAIL

1 tsp. Mr. Boston Crème de Menthe (Green)
1 tsp. Chartreuse (Green)
2 oz. Irish Whisky

Stir with ice and strain into cocktail glass. Serve with a green olive.

EYE-OPENER
1 Egg Yolk
½ tsp. Powdered Sugar
1 tsp. Absinthe Substitute
1 tsp. Mr. Boston Triple Sec
1 tsp. Mr. Boston Crème de Cacao (White)
2 oz. Mr. Boston Rum
Shake with ice and strain into flip glass.

F

FAIR-AND-WARMER COCKTAIL

$3/4$ oz.   Sweet Vermouth
$1^1/2$ oz. Mr. Boston Rum
$1/2$ tsp. Mr. Boston Triple Sec

Stir with ice and strain into cocktail glass.

FAIRY BELLE COCKTAIL

1 Egg White
1 tsp.   Grenadine
$3/4$ oz.   Mr. Boston Apricot Flavored Brandy
$1^1/2$ oz. Mr. Boston Gin

Shake with ice and strain into cocktail glass.

FALLEN ANGEL

Juice of 1 Lime or $1/2$ Lemon
$1^1/2$ oz. Mr. Boston Gin
1 dash Bitters
$1/2$ tsp. Mr. Boston Crème de Menthe (White)

Shake with ice and strain into cocktail glass. Serve with a cherry.

FANCY BRANDY

2 oz.   Mr. Boston Five Star Brandy
1 dash Bitters
$1/4$ tsp. Mr. Boston Triple Sec
$1/4$ tsp. Powdered Sugar

Shake with ice and strain into cocktail glass. Add a twist of lemon peel.

FANCY GIN

Same as Fancy Brandy but made with 2 oz. Mr. Boston Gin.

FANCY WHISKEY

Same as Fancy Brandy but made with 2 oz. Old Thompson Blended Whiskey.

FANTASIO COCKTAIL

1 tsp.   Mr. Boston Crème de Menthe (White)
1 tsp.   Maraschino
1 oz.   Mr. Boston Five Star Brandy
$3/4$ oz.   Dry Vermouth

Stir with ice and strain into cocktail glass.

FARE THEE WELL

1 1/2 oz. Mr. Boston Gin
1/2 oz. Dry Vermouth
1 dash Sweet Vermouth
1 dash Mr. Boston Triple Sec

Shake with ice and strain into cocktail glass.

FARMER'S COCKTAIL

1 oz. Mr. Boston Gin
1/2 oz. Dry Vermouth
1/2 oz. Sweet Vermouth
2 dashes Bitters

Stir with ice and strain into cocktail glass.

FAVORITE COCKTAIL

3/4 oz. Mr. Boston Apricot Flavored Brandy
3/4 oz. Dry Vermouth
3/4 oz. Mr. Boston Gin
1/4 tsp. Lemon Juice

Shake with ice and strain into cocktail glass.

FERRARI

1 oz. Amaretto di Saronno
2 oz. Dry Vermouth

Mix in an old-fashioned glass on the rocks and add a lemon twist.

FIFTH AVENUE

1/2 oz. Mr. Boston Crème de Cacao (Brown)
1/2 oz. Mr. Boston Apricot Flavored Brandy
1 tbsp. Light Cream

Pour carefully, in order given, into parfait glass, so that each ingredient floats on preceding one.

FIFTY-FIFTY COCKTAIL

1 1/2 oz. Mr. Boston Gin
1 1/2 oz. Dry Vermouth

Stir with ice and strain into cocktail glass.

FINE-AND-DANDY COCKTAIL

Juice of 1/4 Lemon
1/2 oz. Mr. Boston Triple Sec
1 1/2 oz. Mr. Boston Gin
1 dash Bitters

Shake with ice and strain into cocktail glass. Serve with a cherry.

FINO MARTINI

2 oz. Mr. Boston Gin
2 tsp. Fino Sherry

Stir with ice and strain into cocktail glass. Add a twist of lemon peel.

FIREMAN'S SOUR
Juice of 2 Limes
$^1/_2$ tsp. Powdered Sugar
1 tbsp. Grenadine
2 oz. Mr. Boston Rum
Shake with ice and strain
into delmonico glass. Fill
with carbonated water, if
desired. Decorate with a
half-slice of lemon and a
cherry.

FISH HOUSE PUNCH
Juice of 1 dozen Lemons
Add enough powdered
sugar to sweeten. Pour over
large block of ice in punch
bowl and stir well. Then
add:
   $1^1/_2$ Liters Mr. Boston
      Five Star Brandy
   1 Liter Mr. Boston Peach
      Flavored Brandy
   16 oz. Mr. Boston Rum
   32 oz. Carbonated
      Water
   16 oz. Strong Tea
      (optional)
Stir well and decorate with
fruits in season. Serve in
punch glasses.

FIXES
See Index on page 259 for
complete list of Fix recipes.

FIZZES
See Index on page 259 for
complete list of Fizz
recipes.

FLAMINGO COCKTAIL
Juice of $^1/_2$ Lime
$^1/_2$ oz. Mr. Boston
   Apricot Flavored
   Brandy
$1^1/_2$ oz. Mr. Boston Gin
1 tsp. Grenadine
Shake with ice and strain
into cocktail glass.

FLIPS
See Index on page 259 for
complete list of Flip
recipes.

FLORADORA COOLER
Into collins glass put:
Juice of 1 Lime
$^1/_2$ tsp. Powdered Sugar
1 tbsp. Grenadine
2 oz. Carbonated
   Water
Stir. Fill glass with ice and
add 2 oz. Mr. Boston Dry
Gin. Fill with carbonated
water or ginger ale and stir
again.

FLORIDA
$^1/_2$ oz. Mr. Boston Gin
$1^1/_2$ tsp. Kirschwasser
$1^1/_2$ tsp. Mr. Boston Triple
   Sec
1 oz. Orange Juice
1 tsp. Lemon Juice
Shake with ice and strain
into cocktail glass.

FLYING DUTCHMAN

2 oz. Mr. Boston Gin
1 dash Mr. Boston Triple Sec

Shake with ice and strain into old-fashioned glass over ice cubes.

FLYING GRASSHOPPER

$3/4$ oz. Mr. Boston Crème de Menthe (Green)
$3/4$ oz. Mr. Boston Crème de Cacao (White)
$3/4$ oz. Mr. Boston Vodka

Stir with ice and strain into cocktail glass.

FLYING SCOTCHMAN

1 oz. Sweet Vermouth
1 oz. Desmond & Duff Scotch
1 dash Bitters
$1/4$ tsp. Sugar Syrup

Stir with ice and strain into cocktail glass.

FOG CUTTER

$1^1/2$ oz. Mr. Boston Rum
$1/2$ oz. Mr. Boston Five Star Brandy
$1/2$ oz. Mr. Boston Gin
1 oz. Orange Juice
3 tbsp. Lemon Juice
$1^1/2$ tsp. Orgeat Syrup

Shake all ingredients and strain into collins glass over ice cubes. Top with a teaspoon of sweet sherry.

FOG HORN

Juice of $1/2$ Lime
$1^1/2$ oz. Mr. Boston Gin

Pour into highball glass over ice cubes. Fill with ginger ale. Stir. Add a slice of lime.

FONTAINEBLEAU SPECIAL

1 oz. Mr. Boston Five Star Brandy
1 oz. Mr. Boston Anisette
$1/2$ oz. Dry Vermouth

Shake with ice and strain into cocktail glass.

FORT LAUDERDALE

$1^1/2$ oz. Mr. Boston Rum
$1/2$ oz. Sweet Vermouth
Juice of $1/4$ Orange
Juice of $1/4$ Lime

Shake with ice and strain into old-fashioned glass over ice cubes. Add a slice of orange.

FOX RIVER COCKTAIL

1 tbsp. Mr. Boston Crème de Cacao (Brown)
2 oz. Old Thompson Blended Whiskey
4 dashes Bitters

Stir with ice and strain into cocktail glass.

Devil's Tail

FRANKENJACK COCKTAIL

1 oz.   Mr. Boston Gin
3/4 oz. Dry Vermouth
1/2 oz. Mr. Boston Apricot Flavored Brandy
1 tsp. Mr. Boston Triple Sec

Stir with ice and strain into cocktail glass. Serve with a cherry.

FREE SILVER

Juice of 1/4 Lemon
1/2 tsp. Powdered Sugar
1 1/2 oz. Mr. Boston Gin
1/2 oz. Mr. Boston Dark Rum
1 tbsp. Milk

Shake with ice and strain into collins glass over ice cubes. Add carbonated water.

FREEZE or FRAPPE

Any **Mr. Boston Flavor Liqueur.** Pour over crushed ice in a champagne glass.

FRENCH CONNECTION

1 1/2 oz. Cognac
3/4 oz. Amaretto di Saronno

Serve in an old-fashioned glass over ice.

FRENCH "75"

Juice of 1 Lemon
2 tsp. Powdered Sugar
2 oz.   Mr. Boston Gin

Stir in collins glass. Then add ice cubes; fill with Shadow Creek champagne and stir. Decorate with a slice of lemon or orange and a cherry. Serve with straws.

FRISCO SOUR

Juice of 1/4 Lemon
Juice of 1/2 Lime
1/2 oz. Benedictine
2 oz.   Old Thompson Blended Whiskey

Shake with ice and strain into sour glass. Decorate with slices of lemon and lime.

FROTH BLOWER COCKTAIL

1 Egg White
1 tsp. Grenadine
2 oz.   Mr. Boston Gin

Shake with ice and strain into cocktail glass.

FROUPE COCKTAIL

1 1/2 oz. Sweet Vermouth
1 1/2 oz. Mr. Boston Five Star Brandy
1 tsp. Benedictine

Stir with ice and strain into cocktail glass.

FROZEN APPLE
1½ oz. Applejack
1 tbsp. Lime Juice
1 tsp. Sugar
½ Egg White
Combine ingredients with a cup of crushed ice in an electric blender and blend at low speed. Pour into old-fashioned glass.

FROZEN BERKELEY
1½ oz. Mr. Boston Rum
½ oz. Mr. Boston Five Star Brandy
1 tbsp. Passion Fruit Syrup
1 tbsp. Lemon Juice
Combine ingredients with a half-cup of crushed ice in an electric blender and blend at low speed. Pour into champagne glass.

FROZEN BRANDY and RUM
1½ oz. Mr. Boston Five Star Brandy
1 oz. Mr. Boston Rum
1 tbsp. Lemon Juice
1 Egg Yolk
1 tsp. Powdered Sugar
Combine ingredients with a cup of crushed ice in an electric blender and blend at low speed. Pour into old-fashioned glass.

FROZEN DAIQUIRI
1½ oz. Mr. Boston Rum
1 tbsp. Mr. Boston Triple Sec
1½ oz. Lime Juice
1 tsp. Sugar
1 cup Crushed Ice
Combine ingredients in an electric blender and blend at low speed for five seconds. Then blend at high speed until firm. Pour into champagne glass. Top with a cherry.

FROZEN MARGARITA
1½ oz. Gavilan Tequila
½ oz. Mr. Boston Triple Sec
1 oz. Lemon or Lime Juice
Combine ingredients with a cup of crushed ice in a blender at low speed for five seconds. Then, blend at high speed until firm. Pour into Cocktail glass. Garnish with a slice of lemon or lime.

FROZEN MATADOR
1½ oz. Gavilan Tequila
2 oz.   Pineapple Juice
1 tbsp. Lime Juice

Combine all ingredients
with a cup of crushed ice
in an electric blender.
Blend at low speed and
pour into old-fashioned
glass. Add a pineapple stick.

FROZEN MINT DAIQUIRI
2 oz.   Mr. Boston Rum
1 tbsp. Lime Juice
6 Mint Leaves
1 tsp. Sugar

Combine all ingredients
with a cup of crushed ice
in an electric blender, and
blend at low speed. Pour
into old-fashioned glass.

FROZEN PINEAPPLE DAIQUIRI
1½ oz. Mr. Boston Rum
4 Pineapple Chunks
1 tbsp. Lime Juice
½ tsp. Sugar

Combine all ingredients
with a cup of crushed ice
in an electric blender.
Blend at low speed and
pour into champagne glass.

G

GABLES COLLINS
1 1/2 oz. Mr. Boston Vodka
1 oz. Mr. Boston Crème de Noyaux
1 tbsp. Lemon Juice
1 tbsp. Pineapple Juice
Shake with ice and strain into collins glass over ice cubes. Add carbonated water. Decorate with a slice of lemon and a pineapple chunk.

GAUGUIN
2 oz. Mr. Boston Rum
1 tbsp. Passion Fruit Syrup
1 tbsp. Lemon Juice
1 tbsp. Lime Juice
Combine ingredients with a cup of crushed ice in an electric blender and blend at low speed. Serve in an old-fashioned glass. Top with a cherry.

GENERAL HARRISON'S EGGNOG
1 Whole Egg
1 tsp. Powdered Sugar
Shake with ice and strain into collins glass. Fill glass with claret or sweet cider and stir. Sprinkle nutmeg on top.

GENTLE BEN
1 oz. Mr. Boston Vodka
1 oz. Mr. Boston Gin
1 oz. Gavilan Tequila
Shake all ingredients with ice and pour into collins glass over ice cubes. Fill with orange juice and stir. Decorate with an orange slice and a cherry.

GEORGIA MINT JULEP
2 sprigs Mint Leaves
1 tsp. Powdered Sugar
1 1/2 oz. Mr. Boston Five Star Brandy
1 oz. Mr. Boston Peach Flavored Brandy
Place mint leaves in collins glass with ice. Add 1 teaspoon sugar and a little water. Muddle, then fill with brandy and peach liqueur. Decorate with mint leaves.

GIBSON
See Special Martini Section on pages 204 and 206.

GILROY COCKTAIL
Juice of 1/4 Lemon
1 tbsp. Dry Vermouth
3/4 oz. Mr. Boston Cherry Flavored Brandy
3/4 oz. Mr. Boston Gin
1 dash Orange Bitters
Shake with ice and strain into cocktail glass.

GIMLET
1 oz. Rose's Lime Juice
1 tsp. Powdered Sugar
1 1/2 oz. Mr. Boston Gin
Shake with ice and strain into cocktail glass.

GIN ALOHA
1 1/2 oz. Mr. Boston Gin
1 1/2 oz. Mr. Boston Triple Sec
1 tbsp. Unsweetened Pineapple Juice
1 dash Orange Bitters
Shake with ice and strain into cocktail glass.

GIN AND BITTERS
1/2 tsp. Bitters
Mr. Boston Gin
Put bitters into cocktail glass and revolve glass until it is entirely coated with the bitters. Then fill with gin. (No ice is used in this drink.)

GIN BUCK
Juice of 1/2 Lemon
1 1/2 oz. Mr. Boston Gin
Ginger Ale
Pour ingredients into old-fashioned glass over ice cubes and stir.

GIN COBBLER
1 tsp. Powdered Sugar
2 oz. Carbonated Water
2 oz. Mr. Boston Gin
Dissolve powdered sugar in carbonated water, then fill goblet with ice and add gin. Stir and decorate with fruits in season. Serve with straws.

GIN COCKTAIL
2 oz. Mr. Boston Gin
2 dashes Bitters
Stir with ice and strain into cocktail glass. Serve with a twist of lemon peel.

GIN COOLER
1/2 tsp. Powdered Sugar
Carbonated Water
2 oz. Mr. Boston Gin
Into a collins glass stir powdered sugar with 2 oz. carbonated water. Fill glass with ice and add gin. Fill with carbonated water or ginger ale and stir again. Insert a spiral of orange or lemon peel (or both) and dangle end over rim of glass.

GIN DAISY
Juice of 1/2 Lemon
1/2 tsp. Powdered Sugar
1 tsp. Grenadine
2 oz. Mr. Boston Gin
Shake with ice and strain into stein or metal cup. Add ice cubes and decorate with fruit.

GIN FIX
Juice of $\frac{1}{2}$ Lemon
1 tsp. Powdered Sugar
1 tsp. Water
$2\frac{1}{2}$ oz. Mr. Boston Gin
Mix lemon juice, powdered sugar, and water in a highball glass. Stir and fill glass with ice. Add gin. Stir, add a slice of lemon. Serve with straws.

GIN FIZZ
Juice of $\frac{1}{2}$ Lemon
1 tsp. Powdered Sugar
2 oz. Mr. Boston Gin
Shake with ice and strain into highball glass with two ice cubes. Fill with carbonated water and stir.

GIN HIGHBALL
2 oz. Mr. Boston Gin
Pour into highball glass over ice cubes and fill with ginger ale or carbonated water. Add a twist of lemon peel, if desired, and stir.

GIN and IT
2 oz. Mr. Boston Gin
1 oz. Sweet Vermouth
Stir ingredients in cocktail glass. (No ice is used in this drink.)

GIN MILK PUNCH
1 tsp. Powdered Sugar
2 oz. Mr. Boston Gin
1 cup Milk
Shake with ice, strain into collins glass, and sprinkle nutmeg on top.

GIN RICKEY
Juice of $\frac{1}{2}$ Lime
$1\frac{1}{2}$ oz. Mr. Boston Gin
Pour ingredients into highball glass over ice cubes and fill with carbonated water. Stir. Add a wedge of lime.

GIN SANGAREE
$\frac{1}{2}$ tsp. Powdered Sugar
1 tsp. Water
2 oz. Mr. Boston Gin
Carbonated Water
1 tbsp. Port
Dissolve powdered sugar in water, and add gin. Pour into highball glass over ice cubes. Fill with carbonated water and stir. Float port on top and sprinkle lightly with nutmeg.

GIN and SIN
1 oz. Mr. Boston Gin
1 oz. Lemon Juice
1 tbsp. Orange Juice
1 dash Grenadine
Shake with ice and strain into cocktail glass.

GIN SLING
1 tsp. Powdered Sugar
1 tsp. Water
Juice of $\frac{1}{2}$ Lemon
2 oz. Mr. Boston Gin
Dissolve powdered sugar in water and lemon. Add gin. Pour into old-fashioned glass over ice cubes and stir. Add a twist of orange peel.

GIN SMASH

1 lump Sugar
1 oz.   Carbonated
    Water
4 sprigs Mint
2 oz.   Mr. Boston Gin

Muddle sugar with carbonated water and mint in old-fashioned glass. Add gin and one ice cube. Stir, and decorate with a slice of orange and a cherry. Add a twist of lemon peel.

GIN SOUR

Juice of ½ Lemon
½ tsp.   Powdered Sugar
2 oz.   Mr. Boston Gin

Shake with ice and strain into sour glass. Decorate with half-slice of lemon and a cherry.

GIN SQUIRT

1½ oz. Mr. Boston Gin
1 tbsp. Powdered Sugar
1 tsp.   Grenadine

Stir with ice and strain into highball glass over ice cubes. Fill with carbonated water and stir. Decorate with cubes of pineapple and strawberries.

GIN SWIZZLE

Into collins glass put:
Juice of 1 Lime
1 tsp.   Powdered Sugar
2 oz.   Carbonated
    Water

Fill glass with ice and stir. Then add:

2 dashes Bitters
2 oz.   Mr. Boston Gin

Fill with carbonated water and serve with swizzle stick in collins glass.

GIN THING

1½ oz. Mr. Boston Gin
Juice of ½ Lime

Pour gin and lime juice in highball glass over ice cubes and fill with ginger ale.

GIN TODDY

½ tsp.   Powdered Sugar
2 tsp.   Water
2 oz.   Mr. Boston Gin

In an old-fashioned glass, mix powdered sugar and water. Add gin and one ice cube. Stir and add a twist of lemon peel.

GIN TODDY (HOT)

1 lump Sugar
Boiling Water
2 oz.   Mr. Boston Gin

Put sugar into hot whiskey glass and fill two-thirds with boiling water. Add gin. Stir and decorate with a slice of lemon. Sprinkle nutmeg on top.

GIN and TONIC
2 oz.   Mr. Boston Gin
Tonic

Pour gin into highball glass over ice cubes and fill with tonic water. Stir.

GLÖGG
Pour the following into a kettle:

2 750ml bottles Wine (Port, Balfour Cream Sherry, Claret, Valley Ridge Burgundy, or Madeira)

Insert cheesecloth bag containing:

2 oz.   Dried Orange Peel
2 oz.   Cinnamon Sticks
20 Cardamom Seeds
25 Cloves

and boil slowly for 15 minutes, stirring occasionally. Add 1 lb. each blanched almonds and seedless raisins and continue to boil for additional 15 minutes. Remove kettle from stove and place wire grill containing 1 lb. lump sugar over opening. Pour one **750ml of Mr. Boston Five Star Brandy** over sugar making sure to saturate all of it. Then light sugar with match and let it flame. After sugar has melted, replace kettle cover to extinguish flame. Stir again and remove spice bag. Serve hot in punch cups with a few almonds and raisins.

GLOOM LIFTER
1 oz.   Old Thompson Blended Whiskey
1/2 oz.   Mr. Boston Five Star Brandy
Juice of 1/2 Lemon
1 tbsp. Raspberry Syrup
1/2 tsp. Sugar
1/2 Egg White

Shake with ice and strain into highball glass with ice cubes.

GOD CHILD
1 oz.   Amaretto di Saronno
1 oz.   Mr. Boston Vodka
1 oz.   Heavy Cream

Shake well with cracked ice. Strain and serve in a champagne glass.

GODFATHER
1 1/2 oz. Desmond & Duff Scotch
3/4 oz.   Amaretto di Saronno

Serve in an old-fashioned glass over ice. (**Kentucky Tavern Bourbon** may also be used instead of Scotch.)

GODMOTHER
1 1/2 oz. Mr. Boston Vodka
3/4 oz.   Amaretto di Saronno

Serve in an old-fashioned glass over ice.

GOLDEN CADILLAC

1 oz.   Galliano
2 oz.   Mr. Boston
         Crème de Cacao
         (White)
1 oz.   Light cream

Combine with half-cup of crushed ice in an electric blender at low speed for ten seconds. Strain into champagne glass.

GOLDEN DAWN

1 oz.   Mr. Boston Apple
         Brandy
1/2 oz. Mr. Boston
         Apricot Flavored
         Brandy
1/2 oz. Mr. Boston Gin
1 oz.   Orange Juice

Shake with ice and strain into old-fashioned glass filled with ice cubes. Add 1 teaspoon grenadine.

GOLDEN DAZE

1 1/2 oz. Mr Boston Gin
1/2 oz.   Mr. Boston Peach
          Flavored Brandy
1 oz.   Orange Juice

Shake with ice and strain into cocktail glass.

GOLDEN DREAM

1 tbsp. Orange Juice
1/2 oz. Mr. Boston Triple
         Sec
1 oz.   Galliano
1 tbsp. Light Cream

Shake with ice and strain into cocktail glass.

GOLDEN FIZZ

Juice of 1/2 Lemon
1/2 tbsp. Powdered Sugar
1 1/2 oz. Mr. Boston Gin
1 Egg Yolk

Shake with ice and strain into highball glass. Fill with carbonated water.

GOLDEN FRAPPE

1 cup Orange Juice
2 tbsp. Lemon Juice
1 tsp.   Sugar
1 cup Port

Stir orange juice, lemon juice, and sugar in collins glass. Add crushed ice and port.

GOLDEN FRIENDSHIP

Equal Parts:
Amaretto di Saronno
Sweet Vermouth
Mr. Boston Light Rum

Mix in a collins glass over ice and fill with ginger ale. Garnish with an orange spiral and a cherry.

GOLDEN SLIPPER

3/4 oz. Chartreuse
         (Yellow)
2 oz.   Mr. Boston
         Apricot Flavored
         Brandy

Stir with ice and strain into cocktail glass. Float an unbroken egg yolk on top.

GOLF COCKTAIL

1 1/2 oz. Mr. Boston Gin
3/4 oz.   Dry Vermouth
2 dashes Bitters

Stir with ice and strain into cocktail glass.

God Child

GRAND ROYAL FIZZ

Juice of 1/4 Orange
Juice of 1/2 Lemon
1 tsp. Powdered Sugar
2 oz. Mr. Boston Gin
1/2 tsp. Maraschino
2 tsp. Light Cream

Shake with ice and strain into highball glass over two ice cubes. Fill with carbonated water and stir.

GRAPEFRUIT COCKTAIL

1 oz. Grapefruit Juice
1 oz. Mr. Boston Gin
1 tsp. Maraschino

Shake with ice and strain into cocktail glass. Serve with a cherry.

GRAPEFRUIT NOG

1 1/2 oz. Mr. Boston Five
Star Brandy
1/2 cup Unsweetened
Grapefruit Juice
1 oz. Lemon Juice
1 tbsp. Honey
1 Whole Egg

Blend all ingredients with a cup of crushed ice at low speed and pour into collins glass over ice cubes.

GRAPE VODKA FROTH

1 1/2 oz. Mr. Boston Vodka
1 oz. Grape Juice
1 Egg White
1 oz. Lemon Juice

Shake with ice and strain into old-fashioned glass over ice cubes.

GRASSHOPPER

3/4 oz. Mr. Boston
Crème de Menthe
(Green)
3/4 oz. Mr. Boston
Crème de Cacao
(White)
3/4 oz. Light Cream

Shake with ice and strain into cocktail glass.

GREENBACK

1 1/2 oz. Mr. Boston Gin
1 oz. Mr. Boston
Crème de Menthe
(Green)
1 oz. Lemon Juice

Shake with ice and strain into old-fashioned glass over ice cubes.

GREEN DEVIL

1 1/2 oz. Mr. Boston Gin
1 1/2 oz. Mr. Boston
Crème de Menthe
(Green)
1 tbsp. Lime Juice

Shake with ice and strain into old-fashioned glass over ice cubes. Decorate with mint leaves.

GREEN DRAGON

Juice of 1/2 Lemon
1/2 oz. Kümmel
1/2 oz. Mr. Boston
Crème de Menthe
(Green)
1 1/2 oz. Mr. Boston Gin
4 dashes Orange Bitters

Shake with ice and strain into cocktail glass.

G

GREEN FIZZ
1 tsp. Powdered Sugar
1 Egg White
Juice of 1/2 Lemon
2 oz. Mr. Boston Gin
1 tsp. Mr. Boston
Crème de Menthe
(Green)
Shake with ice and strain into highball glass over two cubes of ice. Fill with carbonated water and stir.

GREEN HORNET (DRY)
2 oz. Mr. Boston Lime
Vodka
Lemon-Lime Soda
Pour lime vodka over ice cubes in a collins glass. Fill with lemon-lime soda, stir, and add a half-slice of lime.

GREEN OPAL
1/2 oz. Mr. Boston Gin
1/2 oz. Mr. Boston
Anisette
1 oz. Absinthe
Substitute
Shake with ice and strain into cocktail glass.

GREEN SWIZZLE
Make same as Gin Swizzle on page 90 and add 1 tablespoon Mr. Boston Crème de Menthe (Green). If desired, rum, brandy, or whiskey may be substituted for the gin.

GRENADINE RICKEY
Juice of 1/2 Lime
1 1/2 oz. Grenadine
Pour into highball glass over ice cubes and fill with carbonated water. Stir. Put a slice of lime in glass.

GREYHOUND
See Salty Dog recipe on page 153. Do not add the salt.

GYPSY COCKTAIL
1 1/2 oz. Sweet Vermouth
1 1/2 oz. Mr. Boston Gin
Stir with ice and strain into cocktail glass. Serve with a cherry.

H

HAIR RAISER
$1^1/_2$ oz. Mr. Boston 100
    Proof Vodka
$^1/_2$ oz. Mr. Boston Rock
    and Rye
1 tbsp. Lemon Juice
Shake with ice and strain
into cocktail glass.

HARLEM COCKTAIL
$^3/_4$ oz. Pineapple Juice
$1^1/_2$ oz. Mr. Boston Gin
$^1/_2$ tsp. Maraschino
Shake with ice and strain
into cocktail glass. Decorate
with two pineapple chunks.

HARVARD COCKTAIL
$1^1/_2$ oz. Mr. Boston Five
    Star Brandy
$^3/_4$ oz. Sweet Vermouth
1 dash Bitters
1 tsp. Grenadine
2 tsp. Lemon Juice
Shake with ice and strain
into cocktail glass.

HARVARD COOLER
$^1/_2$ tsp. Powdered Sugar
2 oz. Carbonated
    Water
2 oz. Mr. Boston Apple
    Brandy
Into collins glass put
powdered sugar and
carbonated water. Stir.
Then add ice cubes and
apple brandy. Fill with
carbonated water or ginger
ale and stir again. Insert a
spiral of orange or lemon
peel (or both) and dangle
end over rim of glass.

HARVEY WALLBANGER
1 oz. Mr. Boston Vodka
4 oz. Orange Juice
$^1/_2$ oz. Galliano
Pour vodka and orange
juice into collins glass over
ice cubes. Stir. Float
Galliano on top.

HASTY COCKTAIL
$^3/_4$ oz. Dry Vermouth
$1^1/_2$ oz. Mr. Boston Gin
$^1/_4$ tsp. Absinthe
    Substitute
1 tsp. Grenadine
Stir with ice and strain into
cocktail glass.

HAVANA COCKTAIL

$1^1/_2$ oz. Pineapple Juice
$^1/_2$ tsp. Lemon Juice
$^3/_4$ oz. Mr. Boston Rum
Shake with ice and strain
into cocktail glass.

HAWAIIAN COCKTAIL

2 oz. Mr. Boston Gin
1 tbsp. Pineapple Juice
$^1/_2$ oz. Mr. Boston Triple
Sec
Shake with ice and strain
into cocktail glass.

HEADLESS HORSEMAN

2 oz. Mr. Boston Vodka
3 dashes Bitters
Pour into collins glass and
add several ice cubes. Fill
with ginger ale and stir.
Decorate with a slice of
orange.

HIGHBALLS

See Index on page 262 for
complete list of Highball
recipes.

HIGHLAND COOLER

$^1/_2$ tsp. Powdered Sugar
2 oz. Carbonated
Water
2 oz. Desmond & Duff
Scotch
Into collins glass, put
powdered sugar and
carbonated water. Stir.
Then add ice cubes and
scotch. Fill with carbonated
water or ginger ale and stir
again. Insert a spiral of
orange or lemon peel (or
both) and dangle end over
rim of glass.

HIGHLAND FLING COCKTAIL

$^3/_4$ oz. Sweet Vermouth
$1^1/_2$ oz. Desmond & Duff
Scotch
2 dashes Orange Bitters
Stir with ice and strain into
cocktail glass. Serve with an
olive.

HILL BILLY HIGHBALL

2 oz. Georgia Moon
Corn Whiskey
Mountain Dew
Pour into highball glass
over ice cubes, add a twist
of lemon peel, and stir.

HOFFMAN HOUSE COCKTAIL

$^3/_4$ oz. Dry Vermouth
$1^1/_2$ oz. Mr. Boston Gin
2 dashes Orange Bitters
Stir with ice and strain into
cocktail glass. Serve with an
olive.

HOKKAIDO COCKTAIL

$1^1/_2$ oz. Mr. Boston Gin
1 oz. Sake
$^1/_2$ oz. Mr. Boston Triple
Sec
Shake with ice and strain
into cocktail glass.

HOLE-IN-ONE

$1^3/_4$ oz. Desmond & Duff
Scotch
$^3/_4$ oz. Vermouth
$^1/_4$ tsp. Lemon Juice
1 dash Orange Bitters
Shake with ice and strain
into cocktail glass.

HOMESTEAD COCKTAIL

$1^1/_2$ oz. Mr. Boston Gin
$^3/_4$ oz. Sweet Vermouth
Stir with ice and strain into
cocktail glass and serve
with a slice of orange.

HONEYMOON COCKTAIL

$^3/_4$ oz. Benedictine
$^3/_4$ oz. Mr. Boston Apple
Brandy
Juice of $^1/_2$ Lemon
1 tsp. Mr. Boston Triple
Sec
Shake with ice and strain
into cocktail glass.

HONOLULU COCKTAIL NO. 1

1 dash Bitters
$^1/_4$ tsp. Orange Juice
$^1/_4$ tsp. Pineapple Juice
$^1/_4$ tsp. Lemon Juice
$^1/_2$ tsp. Powdered Sugar
$1^1/_2$ oz. Mr. Boston Gin
Shake with ice and strain
into cocktail glass.

HONOLULU COCKTAIL NO. 2

$^3/_4$ oz. Mr. Boston Gin
$^3/_4$ oz. Maraschino
$^3/_4$ oz. Benedictine
Stir with ice and strain into
cocktail glass.

HOOT MON COCKTAIL

$^3/_4$ oz. Sweet Vermouth
$1^1/_2$ oz. Desmond & Duff
Scotch
1 tsp. Benedictine
Stir with ice and strain into
cocktail glass. Twist a
lemon peel and drop in
glass.

HOP TOAD

Juice of $^1/_2$ Lime
$^3/_4$ oz. Mr. Boston
Apricot Flavored
Brandy
$^3/_4$ oz. Mr. Boston Rum
Stir with ice and strain into
cocktail glass.

HORSE'S NECK (WITH a KICK)

2 oz. Old Thompson
Blended Whiskey
Ginger Ale
Peel rind of whole lemon
in spiral fashion and put in
collins glass with one end
hanging over the rim. Fill
glass with ice cubes. Add
blended whiskey. Then fill
with ginger ale and stir
well.

HOT BRANDY FLIP

1 Whole Egg
1 tsp. Powdered Sugar
$1^1/_2$ oz. Mr. Boston Five
Star Brandy
Hot Milk
Beat egg, sugar, and
brandy; pour into mug and
fill with hot milk. Stir.
Sprinkle nutmeg on top.

HOT BRICK TODDY

Into hot whiskey glass, put:
- 1 tsp.   Butter
- 1 tsp.   Powdered Sugar
- 3 pinches Cinnamon
- 1 oz.   Hot Water

Dissolve thoroughly. Then add:

    1¹/₂ oz. Old Thompson
      Blended Whiskey
    Fill with boiling water
      and stir.

HOT BUTTERED RUM

- 1 lump of Sugar
  Boiling Water
  Square of Butter
- 2 oz.   Mr. Boston Rum

Put lump of sugar into hot whiskey glass and fill two-thirds with boiling water. Add square of butter and rum. Stir and sprinkle nutmeg on top.

HOT BUTTERED WINE

For each serving heat ¹/₂ cup muscatel and ¹/₄ cup water just to simmering; do not boil. Preheat mug or cup with boiling water. Pour heated wine mixture into mug and add 1 teaspoon butter and 2 teaspoons maple syrup. Stir and sprinkle nutmeg on top. Serve at once.

HOTEL PLAZA COCKTAIL

- ³/₄ oz.   Sweet Vermouth
- ³/₄ oz.   Dry Vermouth
- ³/₄ oz.   Mr. Boston Gin

Stir with ice and strain into cocktail glass. Decorate with a crushed slice of pineapple.

HOT GOLD

- 6 oz.   Very Warm
    Orange Juice
- 3 oz.   Amaretto di
    Saronno

Pour orange juice into a stemmed wine glass or mug. Add **Amaretto di Saronno** and garnish with a cinnamon stick as stirrer.

HOT PANTS

- 1¹/₂ oz. Gavilan Tequila
- ¹/₂ oz.   Mr. Boston
    Peppermint Schnapps
- 1 tbsp. Unsweetened
    Grapefruit Juice
- 1 tsp.   Powdered Sugar

Shake with ice cubes and pour into old-fashioned glass rimmed with salt.

HOT SPRINGS COCKTAIL

- 1¹/₂ oz. Corbet Canyon
    Chenin Blanc Wine
- 1 tbsp. Pineapple Juice
- ¹/₂ tsp. Maraschino
- 1 dash Orange Bitters

Shake with ice and strain into cocktail glass.

H.P.W. COCKTAIL

1 1/2 tsp. Dry Vermouth
1 1/2 tsp. Sweet Vermouth
1 1/2 oz. Mr. Boston Gin
Stir with ice and strain into cocktail glass. Add a twist of orange peel.

HUDSON BAY

1 oz.　　Mr. Boston Gin
1/2 oz.　　Mr. Boston
　　Cherry Flavored
　　Brandy
1 1/2 tsp. 151 Proof Rum
1 tbsp. Orange Juice
1 1/2 tsp. Lime Juice
Shake with ice and strain into cocktail glass.

HULA-HULA COCKTAIL

3/4 oz.　　Orange Juice
1 1/2 oz. Mr. Boston Gin
1/4 tsp. Powdered Sugar
Shake with ice and strain into cocktail glass.

HUMMER

1 oz.　　Expresso® Coffee
　　Liqueur
1 oz.　　Mr. Boston Light
　　Rum
2 large scoops Vanilla Ice
　　Cream
Blend briefly and serve in highball glass.

HUNTSMAN COCKTAIL

1 1/2 oz. Mr. Boston Vodka
1/2 oz.　　Jamaica Rum
Juice of 1/2 Lime
Powdered Sugar to taste
Shake with ice and strain into cocktail glass.

HURRICANE

1 oz.　　Mr. Boston Dark
　　Rum
1 oz.　　Mr. Boston Light
　　Rum
1 tbsp. Passion Fruit
　　Syrup
2 tsp.　　Lime Juice
Shake with ice and strain into cocktail glass.

HYATT'S JAMAICAN BANANA*

1/2 oz.　　Mr. Boston White
　　Rum
1/2 oz.　　Mr. Boston
　　Crème de Cacao
　　(White)
1/2 oz.　　Mr. Boston
　　Crème de Banana
2 scoops Vanilla Ice
　　Cream
1 oz.　　Half-and-Half
1 Whole Banana
Blend, then garnish with 2 slices banana, strawberry, and nutmeg, and serve in a large brandy snifter.

*Hyatt Regency Hotel, Dallas, Texas

I

ICE CREAM FLIP
1 Whole Egg
1 oz.   Maraschino
1 oz.   Mr. Boston Triple Sec
1 small scoop Vanilla Ice Cream

Shake with ice and strain into flip glass. Sprinkle a little nutmeg on top.

IDEAL COCKTAIL
1 oz.   Dry Vermouth
1 oz.   Mr. Boston Gin
1/4 tsp.   Maraschino
1/2 tsp.   Grapefruit or Lemon Juice

Shake with ice and strain into cocktail glass. Serve with a cherry.

IMPERIAL COCKTAIL
1 1/2 oz.   Dry Vermouth
1 1/2 oz.   Mr. Boston Gin
1/2 tsp.   Maraschino
1 dash Bitters

Stir with ice and strain into cocktail glass. Serve with a cherry.

IMPERIAL FIZZ
Juice of 1/2 Lemon
1/2 oz.   Mr. Boston Rum
1 1/2 oz.   Old Thompson Blended Whiskey
1 tsp.   Powdered Sugar

Shake with ice and strain into highball glass. Add two ice cubes. Fill with carbonated water and stir.

INCIDER COCKTAIL
1 1/2 oz.   Old Thompson Blended Whiskey
Apple Cider

Mix blended whiskey with a generous helping of apple cider. Serve over ice in old-fashioned glass and garnish with a slice of apple.

INCOME TAX COCKTAIL
1 1/2 tsp. Dry Vermouth
1 1/2 tsp. Sweet Vermouth
1 oz.   Mr. Boston Gin
1 dash Bitters
Juice of 1/4 Orange

Shake with ice and strain into cocktail glass.

INDIAN SUMMER

Wet flip glass edge and rim and then dip in cinnamon. Add **2 ounces Mr. Boston Apple Schnapps.** Top off with hot apple cider. Add cinnamon stick if desired.

IRISH COFFEE

1¹/₂ oz. Irish Whisky
Hot Black Coffee
Sugar
Whipped cream

Into a stemmed glass or cup rimmed with sugar, pour Irish whisky. Fill to within ¹/₂ inch of top with coffee. Cover surface to brim with chilled whipped cream.

IRISH RICKEY

Juice of ¹/₂ Lime
Carbonated Water
1¹/₂ oz. Irish Whisky

Pour into highball glass over ice cubes. Stir. Add a piece of lime.

IRISH SHILLELAGH

Juice of ¹/₂ Lemon
1 tsp.   Powdered Sugar
1¹/₂ oz. Irish Whisky
1 tbsp. Mr. Boston Sloe Gin
1 tbsp. Mr. Boston Rum

Shake with ice and strain into punch glass. Decorate with fresh raspberries, strawberries, a cherry, and two peach slices.

IRISH WHISKY

¹/₂ tsp. Mr. Boston Triple Sec
¹/₂ tsp. Absinthe Substitute
¹/₄ tsp. Maraschino
1 dash Bitters
2 oz.   Irish Whisky

Stir with ice and strain into cocktail glass. Serve with an olive.

IRISH WHISKY HIGHBALL

2 oz.   Irish Whisky
Ginger Ale

Pour Irish whisky into highball glass over ice cubes and fill with ginger ale or carbonated water. Add a twist of lemon peel, if desired, and stir.

ITALIAN COFFEE
1½ oz. Amaretto di
   Saronno
Hot Coffee
1½ tbsp. Coffee Ice
   Cream
Ground Coriander

Pour **Amaretto di Saronno** into a heat-resistant stemmed glass or mug. Fill with hot coffee. Top with coffee ice cream. Sprinkle with coriander.

ITALIAN SOMBRERO
1½ oz. Amaretto di
   Saronno
3 oz.   Light Cream

Put in a blender or shake well. Serve over ice cubes or straight up in a champagne glass.

J

JACK-IN-THE-BOX
1 oz.   Mr. Boston Apple
         Brandy
1 oz.   Pineapple Juice
1 dash   Bitters
Shake with ice and strain
into cocktail glass.

JACK ROSE COCKTAIL
1 1/2 oz. Mr. Boston Apple
         Brandy
Juice of 1/2 Lime
1 tsp.   Grenadine
Shake with ice and strain
into cocktail glass.

JADE
1 1/2 oz. Mr. Boston Rum
         (Dark)
1/2 tsp. Mr. Boston
         Crème de Menthe
         (Green)
1/2 tsp. Mr. Boston Triple
         Sec
1 tbsp. Lime Juice
1 tsp.   Powdered Sugar
Shake with ice and strain
into cocktail glass. Add a
lime slice.

JAMAICA COFFEE
1 oz.   Mr. Boston
         Coffee Flavored Brandy
3/4 oz. Mr. Boston Rum
Hot Coffee
Serve in mug, slightly
sweetened. Top with
whipped cream and
sprinkle with nutmeg.

JAMAICA GLOW
1 oz.   Mr. Boston Dry
         Gin
1 tbsp. Claret
1 tbsp. Orange Juice
1 tsp.   Jamaica Rum
Shake with ice and strain
into cocktail glass.

JAMAICA GRANITO
1 small scoop Lemon or
         Orange Sherbet
1 1/2 oz. Mr. Boston Five
         Star Brandy
1 oz.   Mr. Boston Triple
         Sec
Carbonated Water
Combine in collins glass
and stir. Sprinkle nutmeg
on top.

Pink Squirrel and Grasshopper

JAMAICA HOP
1 oz.   Mr. Boston
         Coffee Flavored Brandy
1 oz.   Mr. Boston
         Crème de Cacao
         (White)
1 oz.   Light Cream
Shake well with ice and
strain into cocktail glass.

JAPANESE
2 oz.   Mr. Boston Five
         Star Brandy
1½ tsp. Orgeat Syrup
1 tbsp. Lime Juice
1 dash   Bitters
Shake with ice and strain
into cocktail glass. Add
twist of lime peel.

JAPANESE FIZZ
Juice of ½ Lemon
1 tsp.   Powdered Sugar
1½ oz.   Old Thompson
         Blended Whiskey
1 tbsp. Port
1 Egg White
Shake with ice and strain
into highball glass over two
cubes of ice. Fill with
carbonated water and stir.
Serve with slice of
pineapple.

JEAN LAFITTE
COCKTAIL
1 oz.   Mr. Boston Gin
½ oz.   Mr. Boston Triple
         Sec
½ oz.   Absinthe
         Substitute
1 tsp.   Powdered Sugar
1 Egg Yolk
Shake with ice and strain
into cocktail glass.

JERSEY LIGHTNING
1½ oz.   Mr. Boston Apple
         Brandy
½ oz.   Sweet Vermouth
Juice of 1 lime
Shake with ice and strain
into cocktail glass.

JEWEL COCKTAIL
¾ oz.   Chartreuse
         (Green)
¾ oz.   Sweet Vermouth
¾ oz.   Mr. Boston Gin
1 dash   Orange Bitters
Stir with ice and strain into
cocktail glass. Serve with a
cherry.

JEYPLAK COCKTAIL
1½ oz.   Mr. Boston Gin
¾ oz.   Sweet Vermouth
¼ tsp.   Absinthe
         Substitute
Stir with ice and strain into
cocktail glass. Serve with a
cherry.

JOCKEY CLUB COCKTAIL

1 dash Bitters
$^1/_4$ tsp. Mr. Boston Crème de Cacao (White)
Juice of $^1/_4$ Lemon
$1^1/_2$ oz. Mr. Boston Gin

Shake with ice and strain into cocktail glass.

JOCOSE JULEP

$2^1/_2$ oz. Kentucky Tavern Bourbon
$^1/_2$ oz. Mr. Boston Crème de Menthe (Green)
1 oz. Lime Juice
1 tsp. Sugar
5 Chopped Mint Leaves

Combine all ingredients in an electric blender without ice. Pour into collins glass over ice cubes. Fill with carbonated water and decorate with a sprig of mint.

JOHN COLLINS

Juice of $^1/_2$ Lemon
1 tsp. Powdered Sugar
2 oz. Old Thompson Blended Whiskey

Shake with ice and strain into collins glass. Add several cubes of ice, fill with carbonated water, and stir. Decorate with slices of orange and lemon, and a cherry. Serve with straws.

JOHNNIE COCKTAIL

$^3/_4$ oz. Mr. Boston Triple Sec
$1^1/_2$ oz. Mr. Boston Sloe Gin
1 tsp. Mr. Boston Anisette

Shake with ice and strain into cocktail glass.

JOULOUVILLE

1 oz. Mr. Boston Gin
$^1/_2$ oz. Mr. Boston Apple Brandy
$1^1/_2$ tsp. Sweet Vermouth
1 tbsp. Lemon Juice
2 dashes Grenadine

Shake with ice and strain into cocktail glass.

JOURNALIST COCKTAIL

$1^1/_2$ tsp. Dry Vermouth
$1^1/_2$ tsp. Sweet Vermouth
$1^1/_2$ oz. Mr. Boston Gin
$^1/_2$ tsp. Lemon Juice
$^1/_2$ tsp. Mr. Boston Triple Sec
1 dash Bitters

Shake with ice and strain into cocktail glass.

JUDGE JR. COCKTAIL
$^3/_4$ oz.   Mr. Boston Gin
$^3/_4$ oz.   Mr. Boston Rum
Juice of $^1/_4$ Lemon
$^1/_2$ tsp. Powdered Sugar
$^1/_4$ tsp. Grenadine
Shake with ice and strain
into cocktail glass.

JUDGETTE COCKTAIL
$^3/_4$ oz.   Mr. Boston Peach
    Flavored Brandy
$^3/_4$ oz.   Mr. Boston Gin
$^3/_4$ oz.   Dry Vermouth
Juice of $^1/_4$ Lime
Shake with ice and strain
into cocktail glass. Serve
with a cherry.

JULEPS
See Index on page 262 for
complete list of Julep
recipes.

K

KAMIKAZE
1 oz. Lime Juice
1 oz. Mr. Boston Triple Sec
1 oz. Mr. Boston Vodka
Shake and serve over ice in old-fashioned glass.

KANGAROO COCKTAIL
1 1/2 oz. Mr. Boston Vodka
3/4 oz. Dry Vermouth
Shake with ice and strain into cocktail glass. Serve with a twist of lemon peel.

K.C.B. COCKTAIL
1/2 oz. Kümmel
1 1/2 oz. Mr. Boston Gin
1/4 tsp. Mr. Boston Apricot Flavored Brandy
1/4 tsp. Lemon Juice
Shake with ice and strain into cocktail glass. Add a twist of lemon peel.

KENTUCKY COCKTAIL
3/4 oz. Pineapple Juice
1 1/2 oz. Kentucky Tavern Bourbon
Shake with ice and strain into cocktail glass.

KENTUCKY COLONEL COCKTAIL
1/2 oz. Benedictine
1 1/2 oz. Kentucky Tavern Bourbon
Stir with ice and strain into cocktail glass. Add a twist of lemon peel.

KING COLE COCKTAIL
1 slice Orange
1 slice Pineapple
1/2 tsp. Powdered Sugar
Muddle well in old-fashioned glass and add:
2 oz. Old Thompson Blended Whiskey
2 Ice Cubes
Stir well.

KIR
3 oz. Corbet Canyon Chenin Blanc Wine
3/4 oz. Mr. Boston Crème de Cassis
Pour wine over ice in an old-fashioned glass. Add crème de cassis, a twist of lemon and stir.

KIR ROYALE
- 8 oz.   Shadow Creek Champagne
- Splash Mr. Boston Crème de Cassis

Serve in a large champagne or wine glass.

KISS-IN-THE-DARK
- 3/4 oz.   Mr. Boston Gin
- 3/4 oz.   Mr. Boston Cherry Flavored Brandy
- 3/4 oz.   Dry Vermouth

Stir with ice and strain into cocktail glass.

KISS THE BOYS GOODBYE
- 3/4 oz.   Mr. Boston Sloe Gin
- 3/4 oz.   Mr. Boston Five Star Brandy
- 1/2 Egg White
- Juice of 1 Lemon

Shake with ice and strain into cocktail glass.

KLONDIKE COOLER
- 1/2 tsp.   Powdered Sugar
- 2 oz.   Carbonated Water
- 2 oz.   Old Thompson Blended Whiskey
- Ginger Ale

Into collins glass, mix powdered sugar and carbonated water. Fill glass with ice and add blended whiskey. Fill with carbonated water or ginger ale and stir again. Insert a spiral of orange or lemon peel (or both) and dangle end over rim of glass.

KNICKERBOCKER COCKTAIL
- 1/4 tsp.   Sweet Vermouth
- 3/4 oz.   Dry Vermouth
- 1 1/2 oz.   Mr. Boston Gin

Stir with ice and strain into cocktail glass. Add a twist of lemon peel.

KNICKERBOCKER SPECIAL COCKTAIL
- 1 tsp.   Raspberry Syrup
- 1 tsp.   Lemon Juice
- 1 tsp.   Orange Juice
- 2 oz.   Mr. Boston Rum
- 1/2 tsp.   Mr. Boston Triple Sec

Shake with ice and strain into cocktail glass. Decorate with a small slice of pineapple.

KNOCK-OUT COCKTAIL
- 1/2 oz.   Absinthe Substitute
- 3/4 oz.   Mr. Boston Gin
- 3/4 oz.   Dry Vermouth
- 1 tsp.   Mr. Boston Crème de Menthe (White)

Stir with ice and strain into cocktail glass. Serve with a cherry.

KRETCHMA COCKTAIL

1 oz. Mr. Boston Vodka
1 oz. Mr. Boston
Crème de Cacao
(White)
1 tbsp. Lemon Juice
1 dash Grenadine

Shake with ice and strain
into cocktail glass.

KUP'S INDISPENSABLE COCKTAIL

½ oz. Light Vermouth
½ oz. Dry Vermouth
1½ oz. Mr. Boston Gin
1 dash Bitters

Stir with ice and strain into
cocktail glass.

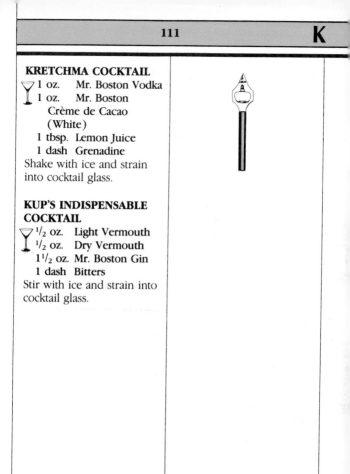

L

LADIES COCKTAIL
$1^3/_4$ oz. Old Thompson
Blended Whiskey
$^1/_2$ tsp. Mr. Boston
Anisette
2 dashes Bitters
Stir with ice and strain into
cocktail glass. Serve with a
pineapple stick on top.

LADY BE GOOD
$1^1/_2$ oz. Mr. Boston Five
Star Brandy
$^1/_2$ oz. Mr. Boston
Crème de Menthe
(White)
$^1/_2$ oz. Sweet Vermouth
Shake with ice and strain
into cocktail glass.

LADY FINGER
1 oz. Mr. Boston Gin
$^1/_2$ oz. Kirschwasser
1 oz. Mr. Boston
Cherry Flavored
Brandy
Shake with ice and strain
into cocktail glass.

LADY LOVE FIZZ
1 tsp. Powdered Sugar
Juice of $^1/_2$ Lemon
1 Egg White
2 oz. Mr. Boston Gin
2 tsp. Light Cream
Shake with ice and strain
into cocktail glass over two
ice cubes. Fill with
carbonated water and stir.

LA JOLLA
$1^1/_2$ oz. Mr. Boston Five
Star Brandy
$^1/_2$ oz. Mr. Boston
Crème de Banana
1 tsp. Orange Juice
2 tsp. Lemon Juice
Shake with ice and strain
into cocktail glass.

LASKY COCKTAIL
$^3/_4$ oz. Grape Juice
$^3/_4$ oz. Swedish Punch
$^3/_4$ oz. Mr. Boston Gin
Shake with ice and strain
into cocktail glass.

LAWHILL COCKTAIL
- 3/4 oz. Dry Vermouth
- 1 1/2 oz. Old Thompson Blended Whiskey
- 1/4 tsp. Absinthe Substitute
- 1/4 tsp. Maraschino
- 1 dash Bitters

Stir with ice and strain into cocktail glass.

LEAP FROG HIGHBALL
- Juice of 1/2 Lemon
- 2 oz. Mr. Boston Gin

Pour into highball glass over ice cubes and fill with ginger ale. Stir.

LEAP YEAR COCKTAIL
- 1 1/4 oz. Mr. Boston Gin
- 1/2 oz. Mr. Boston Orange Flavored Gin
- 1/2 oz. Sweet Vermouth
- 1/4 tsp. Lemon Juice

Shake with ice and strain into cocktail glass.

LEAVE-IT-TO-ME COCKTAIL NO. 1
- 1/2 oz. Mr. Boston Apricot Flavored Brandy
- 1/2 oz. Dry Vermouth
- 1 oz. Mr. Boston Gin
- 1/4 tsp. Lemon Juice
- 1/4 tsp. Grenadine

Shake with ice and strain into cocktail glass.

LEAVE-IT-TO-ME COCKTAIL NO. 2
- 1 tsp. Raspberry Syrup
- 1 tsp. Lemon Juice
- 1/4 tsp. Maraschino
- 1 1/2 oz. Mr. Boston Gin

Stir with ice and strain into cocktail glass.

LEMONADE (CARBONATED)
- 2 tsp. Powdered Sugar
- Juice of 1 Lemon

Dissolve in collins glass, then add ice and enough carbonated water to fill glass and stir. Decorate with slices of orange and lemon, and a cherry. Serve with straws.

LEMONADE (CLARET)
- 2 tsp. Powdered Sugar
- Juice of 1 Lemon
- Water
- 2 oz. Claret

Dissolve sugar and lemon in collins glass, then add ice and enough water to fill glass, leaving room to float claret. Decorate with slices of orange and lemon, and a cherry. Serve with straws.

LEMONADE (EGG)
- Juice of 1 Lemon
- 2 tsp. Powdered Sugar
- 1 Whole Egg

Shake and strain into collins glass over ice cubes. Add enough water to fill glass. Serve with straws.

LEMONADE (FRUIT)
Juice of 1 Lemon
2 tsp.   Powdered Sugar
1 oz.   Raspberry Syrup
Combine in collins glass. Add ice cubes and enough water to fill glass and stir. Decorate with slices of orange and lemon, and a cherry. Serve with straws.

LEMONADE (GOLDEN)
Juice of 1 Lemon
2 tsp.   Powdered Sugar
1 Egg Yolk
6 oz. Water
Shake with ice and strain into collins glass. Decorate with slices of orange and lemon, and a cherry.

LEMONADE (MODERN)
1 Lemon
2 tsp.   Powdered Sugar
1½ oz.   Dry Sherry
1 oz.   Mr. Boston Sloe Gin
Cut lemon into quarters and muddle well with sugar. Add sherry and sloe gin. Shake with ice and strain into collins glass. Fill glass with carbonated water.

LEMONADE (PLAIN)
2 tsp.   Powdered Sugar
Juice of 1 Lemon
Stir. Then fill collins glass with ice. Add enough water to fill glass and stir well. Decorate with slices of orange and lemon and a cherry.

LEMON SQUASH
1 Lemon, peeled and quartered
2 tsp.   Powdered Sugar
Muddle well in collins glass until juice is well extracted. Then fill glass with ice. Add carbonated water and stir. Decorate with fruits.

LIBERTY COCKTAIL
¾ oz.   Mr. Boston Rum
1½ oz.   Mr. Boston Apple Brandy
¼ tsp. Sugar Syrup
Stir with ice and strain into cocktail glass.

LIL NAUE
1 oz.   Mr. Boston Five Star Brandy
½ oz.   Port
½ oz.   Mr. Boston Apricot Flavored Brandy
1 tsp.   Powdered Sugar
1 Egg Yolk
Shake with ice and strain into wine glass. Sprinkle cinnamon on top.

LIMEADE
Juice of 3 Limes
3 tsp.   Powdered Sugar
Combine in collins glass, then add ice and enough water to fill glass. Stir and add a wedge of lime and a cherry in glass. Serve with straws.

LIME GIANT
2 oz.　　Mr. Boston Lime
　　Vodka
Lemon/Lime Soda
Put ice cubes in collins glass and add lime vodka. Fill with lemon and lime soda. Decorate with a slice of lime.

LIMESTONE
1¹/₂ oz. Yellowstone
　　Bourbon
Collins Mix
Lime Juice
In ice-filled highball glass, pour bourbon, fill glass with collins mix and add lime juice to taste.

LIMEY
1 oz.　　Mr. Boston Rum
1 oz.　　Lime Liqueur
¹/₂ oz.　Mr. Boston Triple
　　Sec
2 tsp.　　Lime Juice
Combine ingredients and a half-cup of crushed ice in an electric blender. Blend at low speed and pour into champagne glass. Add a twist of lime peel.

LINSTEAD COCKTAIL
1 oz.　　Old Thompson
　　Blended Whiskey
1 oz.　　Pineapple Juice
¹/₂ tsp. Powdered Sugar
¹/₄ tsp. Absinthe
　　Substitute
¹/₄ tsp. Lemon Juice
Shake with ice and strain into cocktail glass.

LITTLE DEVIL COCKTAIL
Juice of ¹/₄ Lemon
1¹/₂ tsp. Mr. Boston Triple
　　Sec
³/₄ oz.　Mr. Boston Rum
³/₄ oz.　Mr. Boston Gin
Shake with ice and strain into cocktail glass.

LITTLE PRINCESS COCKTAIL
1¹/₂ oz. Sweet Vermouth
1¹/₂ oz. Mr. Boston Rum
Stir with ice and strain into cocktail glass.

LONDON BUCK
2 oz.　　Mr. Boston Gin
Juice of ¹/₂ Lemon
Ginger Ale
Pour over ice cubes in highball glass and stir.

LONDON COCKTAIL
2 oz.　　Mr. Boston Gin
2 dashes Orange Bitters
¹/₂ tsp. Sugar Syrup
¹/₂ tsp. Maraschino
Stir with ice and strain into cocktail glass. Add a twist of lemon peel.

LONDON SPECIAL
Put a large twist of orange peel into champagne glass. Add 1 lump sugar and 2 dashes bitters. Fill with well-chilled Shadow Creek champagne and stir.

LONE TREE COCKTAIL
³/₄ oz.　Sweet Vermouth
1¹/₂ oz. Mr. Boston Gin
Stir with ice and strain into cocktail glass.

LONE TREE COOLER
Into collins glass, put:
- 1/2 tsp. Powdered Sugar
- 2 oz. Carbonated Water

Stir and fill glass with ice and add:
- 2 oz. Mr. Boston Gin
- 1 tbsp. Dry Vermouth

Fill with carbonated water or ginger ale and stir again. Insert a spiral of orange or lemon peel (or both) and dangle end over rim of glass.

LONG ISLAND ICED TEA
Equal parts:
- Mr. Boston Rum
- Mr. Boston Gin
- Mr. Boston Vodka
- Mr. Boston Triple Sec
- Lemon Juice
- Orange Juice

Mix in a highball glass over ice and add a dash of cola.

LOOK OUT BELOW
- 1 1/2 oz. 151 Proof Rum
- Juice of 1/4 Lime
- 1 tsp. Grenadine

Shake with ice and strain into old-fashioned glass over ice cubes.

LOS ANGELES COCKTAIL
- Juice of 1/2 Lemon
- 1 tsp. Powdered Sugar
- 1 Whole Egg
- 1/4 tsp. Sweet Vermouth
- 1 1/2 oz. Old Thompson Blended Whiskey

Shake with ice and strain into flip glass.

LOVE COCKTAIL
- 2 oz. Mr. Boston Sloe Gin
- 1 Egg White
- 1/2 tsp. Lemon Juice
- 1/2 tsp. Raspberry Juice

Shake with ice and strain into cocktail glass.

LOVING CUP
- 4 tsp. Powdered Sugar
- 6 oz. Carbonated Water
- 1 oz. Mr. Boston Triple Sec
- 2 oz. Mr. Boston Five Star Brandy
- 16 oz. Claret

Fill large glass pitcher with ice and stir in the ingredients above. Decorate with fruits in season and also rind of cucumber inserted on each side of pitcher. Top with a small bunch of mint sprigs.

Long Island Iced Tea

LUGGER
- 1 oz.   Mr. Boston Five Star Brandy
- 1 oz.   Mr. Boston Apple Brandy
- 1 dash Mr. Boston Apricot Flavored Brandy

Shake with ice and strain into cocktail glass.

LUXURY COCKTAIL
- 3 oz.   Mr. Boston Five Star Brandy
- 2 dashes Orange Bitters
- 3 oz.   Well-Chilled Shadow Creek Champagne

Stir and pour into champagne glass.

M

MAIDEN'S BLUSH COCKTAIL

- ¼ tsp. Lemon Juice
- 1 tsp. Mr. Boston Triple Sec
- 1 tsp. Grenadine
- 1½ oz. Mr. Boston Gin

Shake with ice and strain into cocktail glass.

MAIDEN'S PRAYER

- 1½ oz. Mr. Boston Gin
- ½ oz. Mr. Boston Triple Sec
- 1 oz. Lemon Juice

Shake with ice and strain into cocktail glass.

MAI-TAI

- ½ tsp. Powdered Sugar
- 2 oz. Mr. Boston Rum
- 1 oz. Mr. Boston Triple Sec
- 1 tbsp. Orgeat or Almond Flavored Syrup
- 1 tbsp. Grenadine
- 1 tbsp. Lime Juice

Shake with ice and strain into large old-fashioned glass about 1/3 full with crushed ice. Decorate with a maraschino cherry speared to a wedge of fresh pineapple. For a hair raiser, top with a dash of 151 proof rum; for a true Hawaiian effect float an orchid on each drink. Serve with straws.

MAJOR BAILEY

- 1½ tsp. Lime Juice
- 1½ tsp. Lemon Juice
- ½ tsp. Powdered Sugar
- 12 Mint Leaves
- 2 oz. Mr. Boston Gin

Muddle first four ingredients well, pour into collins glass filled with ice and add gin. Stir until glass is frosted. Decorate with sprig of mint and serve with straws.

MALMAISON
Juice of $^1/_2$ Lemon
1 oz.　Mr. Boston Rum
$^1/_2$ oz.　Balfour Cream
　　　Sherry
Shake with ice and strain
into cocktail glass rimmed
with **Mr. Boston Anisette**.

MAMIE GILROY
Juice of $^1/_2$ Lime
2 oz.　Desmond & Duff
　　　Scotch
　Ginger Ale
Fill in a collins glass with
ice. Stir.

MAMIE'S SISTER
Juice of 1 Lime
2 oz.　Mr. Boston Gin
　Ginger Ale
Add the juice of one lime
and rind in collins glass,
and add gin. Fill glass with
ginger ale and ice. Stir.

MANDARINE MIST
Pack an old-fashioned glass
with finely crushed ice. Add
$1^1/_2$ oz. Mandarine
Napoleon Liqueur and a
twist of tangerine peel.
Serve with short straws.

MANDARINE SOUR
2 oz.　Mandarine
　　　Napoleon Liqueur
1 oz.　Lemon Juice
Shake with ice and strain
into a sour glass. Decorate
with a cherry and orange
slice.

MANDEVILLE
$1^1/_2$ oz. Mr. Boston Light
　　　Rum
1 oz.　Mr. Boston Dark
　　　Rum
1 tsp.　Absinthe
　　　Substitute
1 tbsp.　Lemon Juice
1 tbsp.　Cola
$^1/_4$ tsp.　Grenadine
Shake with ice and strain
into old-fashioned glass
over ice cubes.

MANHASSET
$1^1/_2$ oz. Old Thompson
　　　Blended Whiskey
$1^1/_2$ tsp. Dry Vermouth
$1^1/_2$ tsp. Sweet Vermouth
1 tbsp.　Lemon Juice
Shake with ice and strain
into cocktail glass.

MANHATTAN
$^3/_4$ oz.　Sweet Vermouth
$1^1/_2$ oz. Old Thompson
　　　Blended Whiskey
Stir with ice and strain into
cocktail glass. Serve with a
cherry.

MANHATTAN (DRY)
$^3/_4$ oz.　Dry Vermouth
$1^1/_2$ oz. Old Thompson
　　　Blended Whiskey
Stir with ice and strain into
cocktail glass. Serve with an
olive.

MANILA FIZZ

2 oz. Mr. Boston Gin
1 Whole Egg
1 tsp. Powdered Sugar
2 oz. Root Beer
Juice of 1 Lime or ½ Lemon

Shake with ice and strain into highball glass over two ice cubes.

MARGARITA

1½ oz. Gavilan Tequila
½ oz. Mr. Boston Triple Sec
1 oz. Lemon or Lime Juice

Rub rim of cocktail glass with rind of lemon or lime, dip rim in salt. Shake ingredients with ice and strain into the salt-rimmed glass.

MARIPOSA

1 oz. Mr. Boston Rum
½ oz. Mr. Boston Five Star Brandy
1 tbsp. Lemon Juice
1 tbsp. Orange Juice
1 dash Grenadine

Shake with ice and strain into cocktail glass.

MARTINEZ COCKTAIL

1 dash Orange Bitters
1 oz. Dry Vermouth
¼ tsp. Mr. Boston Triple Sec
1 oz. Mr. Boston Gin

Stir with ice and strain into cocktail glass. Serve with a cherry.

MARTINI

See Special Martini Section on pages 204 and 206.

MARY GARDEN COCKTAIL

1½ oz. Dubonnet®
¾ oz. Dry Vermouth

Stir with ice and strain into cocktail glass.

MARY PICKFORD COCKTAIL

1 oz. Mr. Boston Rum
1 oz. Pineapple Juice
¼ tsp. Grenadine
¼ tsp. Maraschino

Shake with ice and strain into cocktail glass.

MAURICE COCKTAIL

Juice of ¼ Orange
½ oz. Sweet Vermouth
½ oz. Dry Vermouth
1 oz. Mr. Boston Gin
1 dash Bitters

Shake with ice and strain into cocktail glass.

MAXIM

1½ oz. Mr. Boston Gin
1 oz. Dry Vermouth
1 dash Mr. Boston Crème de Cacao (White)

Shake with ice and strain into cocktail glass.

MAY BLOSSOM FIZZ
1 tsp   Grenadine
Juice of ¹/₂ Lemon
2 oz.   Swedish Punch
Shake with ice and strain into highball glass over two ice cubes. Fill with carbonated water and stir.

McCLELLAND COCKTAIL
³/₄ oz.   Mr. Boston Triple Sec
1¹/₂ oz. Mr. Boston Sloe Gin
1 dash   Orange Bitters
Shake with ice and strain into cocktail glass.

MELON BALL
1 oz.   Melon Liqueur
1 oz.   Mr. Boston Vodka
2 oz.   Pineapple Juice
Pour over ice in a highball glass and garnish with an orange, pineapple, or watermelon slice.

MELON COCKTAIL
2 oz.   Mr. Boston Gin
¹/₄ tsp. Lemon Juice
¹/₄ tsp. Maraschino
Shake with ice and strain into cocktail glass. Serve with a cherry.

MERRY WIDOW COCKTAIL NO. 1
1¹/₄ oz. Mr. Boston Gin
1¹/₄ oz. Dry Vermouth
¹/₂ tsp. Benedictine
¹/₂ tsp. Absinthe Substitute
1 dash   Orange Bitters
Stir with ice and strain into cocktail glass. Add a twist of lemon peel.

MERRY WIDOW COCKTAIL NO. 2
1¹/₄ oz. Maraschino
1¹/₄ oz. Mr. Boston Cherry Flavored Brandy
Stir with ice and strain into cocktail glass. Serve with a cherry.

MERRY WIDOW FIZZ
Juice of ¹/₂ Orange
Juice of ¹/₂ Lemon
1 Egg White
1 tsp.   Powdered Sugar
1¹/₂ oz. Mr. Boston Sloe Gin
Shake with ice and strain into highball glass with two ice cubes. Fill with carbonated water and stir.

METROPOLITAN COCKTAIL
1¹/₄ oz. Mr. Boston Five Star Brandy
1¹/₄ oz. Sweet Vermouth
¹/₂ tsp. Sugar Syrup
1 dash   Bitters
Stir with ice and strain into cocktail glass.

MEXICANA
1½ oz. Gavilan Tequila
1 oz. Lemon Juice
1 tbsp. Pineapple Juice
1 tsp. Grenadine
Shake with ice and strain into cocktail glass.

MEXICAN COFFEE
1 oz. Expresso® Coffee Liqueur
½ oz. Tequila
5 oz. Very Hot Black Coffee
Whipped Cream
Stir coffee liqueur and tequila in coffee cup, add coffee, and top with whipped cream.

MEXICOLA
2 oz. Gavilan Tequila
Juice of ½ Lime
Cola
Fill collins glass with ice cubes. Add tequila and lime juice, fill with cola, and stir.

MIAMI
1½ oz. Mr. Boston Rum
½ oz. Mr. Boston Crème de Menthe (White)
1 dash Lemon Juice
Shake with ice and strain into cocktail glass.

MIAMI BEACH COCKTAIL
¾ oz. Desmond & Duff Scotch
¾ oz. Dry Vermouth
¾ oz. Grapefruit Juice
Shake with ice and strain into cocktail glass.

MIDNIGHT COCKTAIL
1 oz. Mr. Boston Apricot Flavored Brandy
½ oz. Mr. Boston Triple Sec
1 tbsp. Lemon Juice
Shake with ice and strain into cocktail glass.

MIKADO COCKTAIL
1 oz. Mr. Boston Five Star Brandy
1 dash Mr. Boston Triple Sec
1 dash Grenadine
1 dash Mr. Boston Crème de Noyaux
1 dash Bitters
Stir in old-fashioned glass over ice cubes.

MILK PUNCH
1 tsp. Powdered Sugar
2 oz. Old Thompson Blended Whiskey
1 cup Milk
Shake with ice and strain into collins glass. Sprinkle nutmeg on top.

MILLIONAIRE COCKTAIL
1 Egg White
¼ tsp. Grenadine
½ oz. Mr. Boston Triple Sec
1½ oz. Old Thompson Blended Whiskey
Shake with ice and strain into cocktail glass.

MILLION DOLLAR COCKTAIL

2 tsp. Pineapple Juice
1 tsp. Grenadine
1 Egg White
$^3/_4$ oz. Sweet Vermouth
$1^1/_2$ oz. Mr. Boston Gin

Shake with ice and strain into cocktail glass.

MIMOSA

Equal Parts:
Shadow Creek
Champagne
Orange Juice

Serve chilled in a stemmed goblet.

MINT COLLINS

Juice of $^1/_2$ Lemon
2 oz. Mr. Boston Mint
Flavored Gin

Shake with ice and strain into collins glass. Add several ice cubes, fill with carbonated water, and stir. Decorate with slices of lemon and orange, and a cherry. Serve with straws.

MINT GIN COCKTAIL

1 oz. Mr. Boston Mint
Flavored Gin
1 oz. White Port
$1^1/_2$ tsp. Dry Vermouth

Stir with ice and strain into cocktail glass.

MINT HIGHBALL

2 oz. Mr. Boston
Crème de Menthe
(Green)

Pour into highball glass over ice cubes and fill with ginger ale or carbonated water. Add a twist of lemon peel, if desired, and stir.

MINT JULEP

4 sprigs Mint
1 tsp. Powdered Sugar
2 tsp. Water
$2^1/_2$ oz. Kentucky Tavern
Bourbon

Into a silver mug or collins glass muddle mint, powdered sugar, and water. Fill glass or mug with ice and bourbon, and stir until glass is frosted. Decorate with slices of orange, lemon; pineapple, and a cherry. Insert five or six sprigs of mint on top. Serve with straws.

MINT JULEP (SOUTHERN STYLE)

Into a silver mug or collins glass, dissolve one teaspoon powdered sugar with two teaspoons of water. Then fill with finely shaved ice and add 2¹/₂ oz. **Kentucky Tavern Bourbon.** Stir until glass is heavily frosted, adding more ice if necessary. (Do not hold glass with hand while stirring.) Decorate with five or six sprigs of fresh mint so that the tops are about two inches above rim of mug or glass. Use short straws so that it will be necessary to bury nose in mint. The mint is intended for scent rather than taste.

MINT ON ROCKS

Pour 2 oz. Mr. Boston Crème de Menthe (Green) over ice cubes in old-fashioned glass.

MISSISSIPPI PLANTERS PUNCH

1 tbsp. Powdered Sugar
Juice of 1 Lemon
¹/₂ oz. Mr. Boston Rum
¹/₂ oz. Kentucky Tavern Bourbon
1 oz. Mr. Boston Five Star Brandy

Shake all ingredients with ice and strain into collins glass with cubed ice. Fill with carbonated water and stir.

MR. MANHATTAN COCKTAIL

Muddle lump of sugar with:
4 sprigs Mint
¹/₄ tsp. Lemon Juice
1 tsp. Orange Juice
1¹/₂ oz. Mr. Boston Gin

Shake with ice and strain into cocktail glass.

MOCHA MINT

³/₄ oz. Mr. Boston Coffee Flavored Brandy
³/₄ oz. Mr. Boston Crème de Cacao (White)
³/₄ oz. Mr. Boston Crème de Menthe (White)

Shake with ice and strain into cocktail glass.

MODERN COCKTAIL

1¹/₂ oz. Desmond & Duff Scotch
¹/₂ tsp. Lemon Juice
¹/₄ tsp. Absinthe Substitute
¹/₂ tsp. Jamaica Rum
1 dash Orange Bitters

Shake with ice and strain into cocktail glass. Serve with a cherry.

MONTANA

1¹/₂ oz. Mr. Boston Five Star Brandy
1 oz. Port
¹/₂ oz. Dry Vermouth

Stir in old-fashioned glass on the rocks.

Mint Julep

MONTE CARLO IMPERIAL HIGHBALL

2 oz.   Mr. Boston Gin
$^1/_2$ oz.   Mr. Boston
    Crème de Menthe
    (White)
    Juice of $^1/_4$ Lemon

Shake with ice and strain into highball glass over ice cubes. Fill glass with champagne and stir.

MONTEZUMA

$1^1/_2$ oz. Gavilan Tequila
1 oz.   Madeira
1 Egg Yolk
$^1/_2$ cup Crushed Ice

Mix in blender at low speed and serve in champagne glass.

MONTMARTRE COCKTAIL

$1^1/_4$ oz. Mr. Boston Dry
    Gin
$^1/_2$ oz.   Sweet Vermouth
$^1/_2$ oz.   Mr. Boston Triple
    Sec

Stir with ice and strain into cocktail glass. Serve with a cherry.

MONTREAL CLUB BOUNCER

$1^1/_2$ oz. Mr. Boston Gin
$^1/_2$ oz.   Absinthe
    Substitute

Pour into old-fashioned glass over ice cubes. Stir.

MONTREAL GIN SOUR

1 oz.   Mr. Boston Gin
1 oz.   Lemon Juice
$^1/_2$ Egg White
1 tsp.   Powdered Sugar

Shake with ice and strain into sour glass. Add a slice of lemon.

MOONLIGHT

2 oz.   Mr. Boston Apple
    Brandy
    Juice of 1 Lemon
1 tsp.   Powdered Sugar

Shake with ice and strain into old-fashioned glass over ice cubes.

MOON QUAKE SHAKE

$1^1/_2$ oz. Mr. Boston Rum
    (Dark)
1 oz.   Mr. Boston
    Coffee Flavored Brandy
1 tbsp. Lemon Juice

Shake with ice and strain into cocktail glass.

MORNING COCKTAIL

1 oz.   Mr. Boston Five
    Star Brandy
1 oz.   Dry Vermouth
$^1/_4$ tsp. Mr. Boston Triple
    Sec
$^1/_4$ tsp. Maraschino
$^1/_4$ tsp. Absinthe
    Substitute
2 dashes Orange Bitters

Stir with ice and strain into cocktail glass. Serve with a cherry.

MORNING GLORY FIZZ

Juice of $^1/_2$ Lemon or 1
   Lime
1 tsp.   Powdered Sugar
1 Egg White
$^1/_2$ tsp. Absinthe
   Substitute
2 oz.   Desmond & Duff
   Scotch

Shake with ice and strain
into highball glass over two
ice cubes. Fill with
carbonated water and stir.

MORRO

1 oz.   Mr. Boston Gin
$^1/_2$ oz. Mr. Boston Rum
   (Dark)
1 tbsp. Pineapple Juice
1 tbsp. Lime Juice
$^1/_2$ tsp. Powdered Sugar

Shake with ice and strain
into sugar rimmed old-
fashioned glass over ice
cubes.

MOSCOW MULE

Into a copper mug, pour:
$1^1/_2$ oz. Mr. Boston Vodka
   Juice of $^1/_2$ Lime

Add ice cubes and fill with
ginger beer. Drop lime
wedge in mug for
decoration.

MOULIN ROUGE

$1^1/_2$ oz. Mr. Boston Sloe
   Gin
$^3/_4$ oz. Sweet Vermouth
1 dash Bitters

Stir with ice and strain into
cocktail glass.

MOUNTAIN COCKTAIL

1 Egg White
$^1/_4$ tsp. Lemon Juice
$^1/_4$ tsp. Dry Vermouth
$^1/_4$ tsp. Sweet Vermouth
$1^1/_2$ oz. Old Thompson
   Blended Whiskey

Shake with ice and strain
into cocktail glass.

MULLED CLARET

Into a metal mug put:
1 lump Sugar
   Juice of $^1/_2$ Lemon
1 dash Bitters
1 tsp. Mixed Cinnamon
   and Nutmeg
5 oz.   Claret

Heat poker red hot and
hold in liquid until boiling
and serve; or warm on a
stove.

N

NAPOLEON

2 oz.   Mr. Boston Gin
½ tsp. Curaçao
½ tsp. Dubonnet®
Stir with ice and strain into
cocktail glass.

NARRAGANSETT

1½ oz. Kentucky Tavern
          Bourbon
1 oz.   Sweet Vermouth
1 dash Mr. Boston
          Anisette
Stir in old-fashioned glass
with ice cubes. Add a twist
of lemon peel.

NEGRONI

¾ oz.   Mr. Boston Gin
¾ oz.   Campari
¾ oz.   Sweet or Dry
          Vermouth
Stir with ice and strain into
cocktail glass, or into old-
fashioned glass over ice
cubes, with or without a
splash of carbonated water.
Add a twist of lemon peel.

NETHERLAND

1 oz.   Mr. Boston Five
          Star Brandy
1 oz.   Mr. Boston Triple
          Sec
1 dash Orange Bitters
Stir in old-fashioned glass
with ice cubes.

NEVADA COCKTAIL

1½ oz. Mr. Boston Rum
1 oz.   Grapefruit Juice
Juice of 1 Lime
1 dash Bitters
3 tsp.   Powdered Sugar
Shake with ice and strain
into cocktail glass.

NEVINS

1½ oz. Kentucky Tavern
          Bourbon
1½ tsp. Mr. Boston
          Apricot Flavored
          Brandy
1 tbsp. Grapefruit Juice
1½ tsp. Lemon Juice
1 dash Bitters
Shake with ice and strain
into cocktail glass.

NEW ORLEANS BUCK

1½ oz. Mr. Boston Rum
1 oz.   Orange Juice
½ oz.   Lemon Juice

Shake all ingredients with ice and strain into collins glass over ice cubes. Fill with ginger ale and stir.

NEW ORLEANS GIN FIZZ

Juice of ½ Lemon
Juice of ½ Lime
    (optional)
1 tsp.   Powdered Sugar
1 Egg White
2 oz.   Mr. Boston Gin
1 tbsp. Light Cream
½ tsp. Mr. Boston Triple Sec

Shake with ice and strain into highball glass with two ice cubes. Fill with carbonated water and stir.

NEW YORK COCKTAIL

Juice of 1 Lime or ½ Lemon
1 tsp.   Powdered Sugar
1½ oz. Old Thompson Blended Whiskey
½ tsp. Grenadine

Shake with ice and strain into cocktail glass. Add a twist of lemon peel.

NEW YORK SOUR

Juice of ½ Lemon
1 tsp.   Powdered Sugar
2 oz.   Old Thompson Blended Whiskey

Shake with ice and strain into sour glass, leaving about half-inch on which to float claret. Decorate with a half-slice of lemon and a cherry.

NIGHT CAP

2 oz.   Mr. Boston Rum
1 tsp.   Powdered Sugar

Add enough warm milk to fill a mug and stir. Sprinkle a little nutmeg on top.

NIGHTMARE

1½ oz. Mr. Boston Gin
½ oz.   Madeira
½ oz.   Mr. Boston Cherry Flavored Brandy
1 tsp.   Orange Juice

Shake with ice and strain into cocktail glass.

NINOTCHKA COCKTAIL
1 1/2 oz. Mr. Boston Vodka
1/2 oz. Mr. Boston
Crème de Cacao
(White)
1 tbsp. Lemon Juice
Shake with ice and strain
into cocktail glass.

NORTH POLE COCKTAIL
1 Egg White
1/2 oz. Lemon Juice
1/2 oz. Maraschino
1 oz. Mr. Boston Gin
Shake with ice and strain
into cocktail glass. Top with
whipped cream.

NUTTY COLADA
See Saronno Colada recipe
on page 154.

O

OLD-FASHIONED 🥃
Into an old-fashioned glass put a small cube of sugar, a dash of bitters, a teaspoon of water, and muddle well. Add **2 oz. Old Thompson Blended Whiskey**. Stir. Add a twist of lemon peel and ice cubes. Decorate with slices of orange, lemon, and a cherry. Serve with a swizzle stick.

OLD PAL COCKTAIL
🍸 ½ oz. Grenadine
½ oz. Sweet Vermouth
1¼ oz. Old Thompson Blended Whiskey
Stir with ice and strain into cocktail glass.

OLYMPIC COCKTAIL
🍸 ¾ oz. Orange Juice
¾ oz. Mr. Boston Triple Sec
¾ oz. Mr. Boston Five Star Brandy
Shake with ice and strain into cocktail glass.

OPAL COCKTAIL
🍸 1 oz. Mr. Boston Gin
½ oz. Mr. Boston Triple Sec
1 tbsp. Orange Juice
¼ tbsp. Powdered Sugar
Shake with ice and strain into cocktail glass.

OPENING COCKTAIL
🍸 ½ oz. Grenadine
½ oz. Sweet Vermouth
1½ oz. Old Thompson Blended Whiskey
Stir with ice and strain into cocktail glass.

OPERA COCKTAIL
🍸 1 tbsp. Maraschino
½ oz. Dubonnet®
1½ oz. Mr. Boston Gin
Stir with ice and strain into cocktail glass.

ORANGEADE
🥤 Juice of 2 Oranges
1 tsp. Powdered Sugar
Mix in collins glass. Add ice cubes and enough water to fill glass and stir. Decorate with slices of orange and lemon, and two cherries. Serve with straws.

ORANGE BLOSSOM

1 oz.   Mr. Boston Gin
1 oz.   Orange Juice
¼ tsp. Powdered Sugar
Shake with ice and strain
into cocktail glass.

ORANGE BUCK

1½ oz. Mr. Boston Gin
1 oz.   Orange Juice
1 tbsp. Lime Juice
Shake with ice and strain
into highball glass over ice
cubes. Fill with ginger ale
and stir.

ORANGE OASIS

1½ oz. Mr. Boston Gin
½ oz.   Mr. Boston
         Cherry Flavored
         Brandy
4 oz.   Orange Juice
Shake with ice and strain
into highball glass over ice
cubes. Fill with ginger ale
and stir.

ORANGE SMILE

1 Whole Egg
Juice of 1 Large Orange
1 tbsp. Grenadine
Shake with ice and strain
into stem goblet.

ORIENTAL COCKTAIL

1 oz.   Old Thompson
         Blended Whiskey
½ oz.   Sweet Vermouth
½ oz.   Mr. Boston Triple
         Sec
Juice of ½ Lime
Shake with ice and strain
into cocktail glass.

OUTRIGGER

1 oz.   Mr. Boston Peach
         Flavored Brandy
1 oz.   Mr. Boston Lime
         Vodka
1 oz.   Pineapple Juice
Shake with ice and strain
into old-fashioned glass
over ice cubes.

P

PADDY COCKTAIL
1½ oz.   Irish Whisky
1½ oz.   Sweet Vermouth
1 dash Bitters
Stir with ice and strain into cocktail glass.

PAISLEY MARTINI
2 oz.   Mr. Boston Gin
½ oz.   Dry Vermouth
1 tsp.   Desmond & Duff Scotch
Stir in old-fashioned glass over ice cubes. Add a twist of lemon peel.

PALL MALL
1½ oz.   Mr. Boston Gin
½ oz.   Sweet Vermouth
½ oz.   Dry Vermouth
½ oz.   Mr. Boston Crème de Menthe (White)
Stir in old-fashioned glass over ice cubes.

PALM BEACH COCKTAIL
1½ oz.   Mr. Boston Gin
1½ tsp. Sweet Vermouth
1½ tsp. Grapefruit Juice
Shake with ice and strain into cocktail glass.

PALMER COCKTAIL
2 oz.   Old Thompson Blended Whiskey
1 dash Bitters
½ tsp.   Lemon Juice
Stir with ice and strain in cocktail glass.

PALMETTO COCKTAIL
1½ oz.   Mr. Boston Rum
1½ oz.   Dry Vermouth
2 dashes Bitters
Stir with ice and strain into cocktail glass.

PANAMA COCKTAIL
1 oz.   Mr. Boston Crème de Cacao (White)
1 oz.   Light Cream
1 oz.   Mr. Boston Five Star Brandy
Shake with ice and strain into cocktail glass.

PAPAYA SLING
1½ oz.   Mr. Boston Gin
1 dash Bitters
Juice of 1 Lime
1 tbsp. Papaya Syrup
Shake with ice and strain into collins glass over ice cubes. Fill with carbonated water and stir. Add a pineapple stick.

PARADISE COCKTAIL

1 oz. Mr. Boston
  Apricot Flavored
  Brandy
³/₄ oz. Mr. Boston Gin
Juice of ¹/₄ Orange
Shake with ice and strain
into cocktail glass.

PARISIAN

1 oz. Mr. Boston Gin
1 oz. Dry Vermouth
¹/₄ oz. Mr. Boston
  Crème de Cassis
Shake with ice and strain
into cocktail glass.

PARISIAN BLONDE

³/₄ oz. Light Cream
³/₄ oz. Mr. Boston Triple
  Sec
³/₄ oz. Jamaica Rum
Shake with ice and strain
into cocktail glass.

PARK AVENUE

1¹/₂ oz. Mr. Boston Gin
³/₄ oz. Sweet Vermouth
1 tbsp. Pineapple Juice
Stir with ice and strain into
cocktail glass.

PASSION DAIQUIRI

1¹/₂ oz. Mr. Boston Rum
Juice of 1 Lime
1 tsp. Powdered Sugar
1 tbsp. Passion Fruit
  Juice
Shake with ice and strain
into cocktail glass.

PEACH BLOSSOM

1 tsp. Lemon Juice
¹/₂ tsp. Powdered Sugar
2 oz. Mr. Boston Gin
¹/₂ Peach
Shake with ice and strain
into highball glass over ice
cubes. Fill with carbonated
water and stir.

PEACH BLOW FIZZ

Juice of ¹/₂ Lemon
¹/₂ tsp. Powdered Sugar
1 oz. Light Cream
2 oz. Mr. Boston Gin
¹/₄ Peach
Shake with ice and strain
into highball glass over ice
cubes. Fill with carbonated
water and stir.

PEACH BUNNY

³/₄ oz. Mr. Boston Peach
  Flavored Brandy
³/₄ oz. Mr. Boston
  Crème de Cacao
  (White)
³/₄ oz. Light Cream
Shake well with ice and
strain into cocktail glass.

PEACH SANGAREE

2 oz. Mr. Boston Peach
  Flavored Brandy
Carbonated Water
1 tsp. Port
Put brandy into highball
glass with ice cubes. Fill
glass with carbonated
water. Stir and float port on
top. Sprinkle lightly with
nutmeg.

PEGGY COCKTAIL

3/4 oz. Dry Vermouth
1 1/2 oz. Mr. Boston Gin
1/4 tsp. Absinthe
     Substitute
1/4 tsp. Dubonnet®
Stir with ice and strain into cocktail glass.

PENDENNIS TODDY

Muddle a lump of sugar with one teaspoon of water, in sour glass. Fill with ice, add **2 oz. Kentucky Tavern Bourbon** and stir. Decorate with two slices of lemon.

PEPPERMINT ICEBERG

Pour **2 oz. Mr. Boston Peppermint Schnapps** into old-fashioned glass over ice cubes. Stir and serve with a peppermint-candy swizzle stick.

PEPPERMINT PATTIE

1 oz. Mr. Boston
     Crème de Cacao
     (White)
1 oz. Mr. Boston
     Crème de Menthe
     (White)
Shake with ice and strain into old-fashioned glass over ice cubes.

PEPPERMINT STICK

1 oz. Mr. Boston
     Peppermint Schnapps
1 1/2 oz. Mr. Boston
     Crème de Cacao
     (White)
1 oz. Light Cream
Shake with ice and strain into champagne glass.

PERFECT COCKTAIL

1 1/2 tsp. Dry Vermouth
1 1/2 tsp. Sweet Vermouth
1 1/2 oz. Mr. Boston Gin
1 dash Bitters
Stir with ice and strain into cocktail glass.

PETER PAN COCKTAIL

2 dashes Bitters
3/4 oz. Orange Juice
3/4 oz. Dry Vermouth
3/4 oz. Mr. Boston Gin
Shake with ice and strain into cocktail glass.

PHOEBE SNOW

1 1/2 oz. Dubonnet®
1 1/2 oz. Mr. Boston Five
     Star Brandy
1/2 tsp. Absinthe
     Substitute
Stir with ice and strain into cocktail glass.

PICCADILLY COCKTAIL

3/4 oz. Dry Vermouth
1 1/2 oz. Mr. Boston Gin
1/4 tsp. Absinthe
     Substitute
1/4 tsp. Grenadine
Stir with ice and strain into cocktail glass.

PICON COCKTAIL

See Amer Picon Cocktail on page 31.

PIKE'S PEAK COOLER
Juice of $1/2$ Lemon
1 tsp. Powdered Sugar
1 Whole Egg

Shake with ice and strain into collins glass with cracked ice. Fill with cider and stir. Insert a spiral of orange or lemon peel (or both) and dangle end over rim of glass.

PIÑA COLADA
3 oz. Mr. Boston Rum
3 tbsp. Coconut Milk
3 tbsp. Crushed Pineapple

Place in an electric blender with two cups of crushed ice and blend at high speed for a short time. Strain into collins glass and serve with straw.

PINEAPPLE COCKTAIL
$3/4$ oz. Pineapple Juice
$1^1/2$ oz. Mr. Boston Rum
$1/2$ tsp. Lemon Juice

Shake with ice and strain into cocktail glass.

PINEAPPLE COOLER
Into collins glass put:
2 oz. Pineapple Juice
$1/2$ tsp. Powdered Sugar
2 oz. Carbonated Water
2 oz. Corbett Canyon Chenin Blanc Wine

Stir. Add ice cubes. Fill with carbonated water and stir again. Insert a spiral of orange or lemon peel (or both) and dangle end over rim of glass.

PINEAPPLE FIZZ
1 oz. Pineapple Juice
$1/2$ tsp. Powdered Sugar
2 oz. Mr. Boston Rum

Shake with ice and strain into highball glass over two ice cubes. Fill with carbonated water and stir.

PING-PONG COCKTAIL
Juice of $1/4$ Lemon
1 Egg White
2 oz. Mr. Boston Sloe Gin

Shake with ice and strain into cocktail glass.

PINK CREOLE
$1^1/2$ oz. Mr. Boston Rum
1 tbsp. Lime Juice
1 tsp. Grenadine
1 tsp. Light Cream

Shake with ice and strain into cocktail glass. Add a black cherry soaked in rum.

PINK GIN
See Gin and Bitters recipe on page 88.

PINK LADY
1 Egg White
1 tsp. Grenadine
1 tsp. Light Cream
$1^1/2$ oz. Mr. Boston Gin

Shake with ice and strain into cocktail glass.

PINK PUSSY CAT ⬜

Into a highball glass almost filled with ice put 1¹/₂ oz. **Mr. Boston Dry Vodka or Gin.** Fill balance of glass with pineapple or grapefruit juice. Add a dash of grenadine for color and stir.

PINK ROSE FIZZ

☐ Juice of ¹/₂ Lemon
1 tsp.   Powdered Sugar
1 Egg White
2 tsp.   Light Cream
2 oz.   Mr. Boston Gin

Shake with ice and strain into highball glass over two ice cubes. Fill with carbonated water and stir.

PINK SQUIRREL

▽ 1 oz.   Mr. Boston Crème de Noyaux
1 tbsp. Mr. Boston Crème de Cacao (White)
1 tbsp. Light Cream

Shake with ice and strain into cocktail glass.

PLAIN VERMOUTH COCKTAIL

See Vermouth Cocktail page 178.

PLANTER'S COCKTAIL

▽ Juice of ¹/₄ Lemon
¹/₂ tsp. Powdered Sugar
1¹/₂ oz. Jamaica Rum

Shake with ice and strain into cocktail glass.

PLANTER'S PUNCH NO. 1

☐ Juice of 2 Limes
2 tsp.   Powdered Sugar
2 oz.   Carbonated Water

Mix in a collins glass, add ice cubes and stir until glass is frosted. Add two dashes bitters and 2¹/₂ oz. **Mr. Boston Rum.** Stir and decorate with slices of lemon, orange, pineapple, and a cherry. Serve with a straw.

PLANTER'S PUNCH NO. 2

☐ Juice of 1 Lime
Juice of ¹/₂ Lemon
Juice of ¹/₂ Orange
1 tsp.   Pineapple Juice
2 oz.   Mr. Boston Rum

Pour into collins glass, filled well with ice. Stir until glass is frosted. Then add 1 oz. Jamaica rum, stir, and top with 2 dashes Mr. Boston Triple Sec. Decorate with slices of orange, lemon, pineapple, a cherry, and a sprig of mint dipped in powdered sugar. Serve with a straw.

PLAZA COCKTAIL

▽ ³/₄ oz.   Sweet Vermouth
³/₄ oz.   Dry Vermouth
³/₄ oz.   Mr. Boston Gin

Shake with ice and strain into cocktail glass. Add a strip of pineapple.

POKER COCKTAIL
1 1/2 oz. Sweet Vermouth
1 1/2 oz. Mr. Boston Rum
Stir with ice and strain into cocktail glass.

POLLYANNA
Muddle 3 slices of orange and 3 slices of pineapple with:
2 oz. Mr. Boston Gin
1/2 oz. Sweet Vermouth
1/2 tsp. Grenadine
Shake with ice and strain into cocktail glass.

POLO COCKTAIL
1 tbsp. Lemon Juice
1 tbsp. Orange Juice
1 oz. Mr. Boston Gin
Shake with ice and strain into cocktail glass.

POLONAISE
1 1/2 oz. Mr. Boston Five Star Brandy
1 tbsp. Mr. Boston Blackberry Flavored Brandy
1/2 oz. Dry Sherry
1 dash Lemon Juice
Shake with ice and strain into old-fashioned glass over ice cubes.

POLYNESIAN COCKTAIL
1 1/2 oz. Mr. Boston Vodka
3/4 oz. Mr. Boston Cherry Flavored Brandy
Juice of 1 Lime
Rub rim of cocktail glass with lime and dip into powdered sugar. Shake above ingredients with ice and strain into prepared glass.

POMPANO
1 oz. Mr. Boston Gin
1/2 oz. Dry Vermouth
1 oz. Grapefruit Juice
Shake with ice and strain into cocktail glass.

POOP DECK COCKTAIL
1 oz. Mr. Boston Five Star Brandy
1 oz. Port
1 tbsp. Mr. Boston Blackberry Flavored Brandy
Shake with ice and strain into cocktail glass.

POPPY COCKTAIL
3/4 oz. Mr. Boston Crème de Cacao (White)
1 1/2 oz. Mr. Boston Gin
Shake with ice and strain into cocktail glass.

PORT AND STARBOARD
1 tbsp. Grenadine
1/2 oz. Mr. Boston Crème de Menthe (Green)

Pour carefully into pousse-café glass, so that crème de menthe floats on grenadine.

PORT MILK PUNCH
1 tsp. Powdered Sugar
2 oz. Port
1 cup Milk

Shake with ice and strain into collins glass. Sprinkle nutmeg on top.

PORT WINE COBBLER
Dissolve 1 teaspoon powdered sugar in 2 oz. carbonated water; then fill goblet with shaved ice and add 3 oz. port. Stir and decorate with fruits in season. Serve with straws.

PORT WINE COCKTAIL
2 1/2 oz. Port
1/2 tsp. Mr. Boston Five Star Brandy

Stir with ice and strain into cocktail glass.

PORT WINE EGGNOG
1 Whole Egg
1 tsp. Powdered Sugar
3 oz. Port
6 oz. Milk

Shake well with ice and strain into collins glass. Sprinkle nutmeg on top.

PORT WINE FLIP
1 Whole Egg
1 tsp. Powdered Sugar
1 1/2 oz. Port
2 tsp. Light Cream (if desired)

Shake with ice and strain into flip glass. Sprinkle a little nutmeg on top.

PORT WINE NEGUS
1/2 lump Sugar
2 oz. Port

Pour into hot whisky glass, fill with hot water and stir. Sprinkle nutmeg on top.

PORT WINE SANGAREE
Dissolve 1/2 teaspoon powdered sugar in 1 teaspoon water in highball glass. Add 2 oz. port and ice cubes. Fill with carbonated water leaving enough room on which to float a tablespoon of **Mr. Boston Five Star Brandy**. Stir. Float brandy on top. Sprinkle with nutmeg.

POUSSE CAFÉ
Equal parts:
Grenadine
Chartreuse (Yellow)
Mr. Boston Crème de
Cassis
Mr. Boston Crème de
Menthe (White)
Chartreuse (Green)
Mr. Boston Five Star
Brandy

Pour carefully, in order given, into pousse-café glass so that each ingredient floats on preceding one. (For other Pousse Café recipes, see Index on page 263.)

POUSSE L'AMOUR
1 tbsp. Maraschino
1 Egg Yolk
$^1/_2$ oz. Benedictine
$^1/_2$ oz. Mr. Boston Five Star Brandy

Pour carefully, in order given, into 2 oz. sherry glass, so that each ingredient floats on preceding one.

PRADO
$1^1/_2$ oz. Gavilan Tequila
$^3/_4$ oz. Lemon Juice
1 tbsp. Maraschino
$^1/_2$ Egg White
1 tsp. Grenadine

Shake with ice and strain into sour glass. Add a slice of lime and a cherry.

PRAIRIE CHICKEN
1 oz. Mr. Boston Gin
1 Whole Egg
Pepper and Salt

Open egg without breaking the yolk and put in wine glass. Pour gin on top. Add pepper and salt.

PRAIRIE OYSTER
1 oz. Mr. Boston Five Star Brandy
1 tbsp. Worcestershire Sauce
1 tsp. Catsup
1 tbsp. Vinegar
1 pinch Pepper

Shake with ice and strain into old-fashioned glass over two ice cubes. Place an egg yolk on top without breaking it. Add a dash of cayenne pepper.

PREAKNESS COCKTAIL
$^3/_4$ oz. Sweet Vermouth
$1^1/_2$ oz. Old Thompson Blended Whiskey
1 dash Bitters
$^1/_2$ tsp. Benedictine

Stir with ice and strain into cocktail glass. Add a twist of lemon peel.

PRESTO COCKTAIL

1 tbsp. Orange Juice
1/2 oz. Sweet Vermouth
1 1/2 oz. Mr. Boston Five Star Brandy
1/4 tsp. Absinthe Substitute

Shake with ice and strain into cocktail glass.

PRINCE'S SMILE

1/2 oz. Mr. Boston Apricot Flavored Brandy
1/2 oz. Mr. Boston Apple Brandy
1 oz. Mr. Boston Gin
1/4 tsp. Lemon Juice

Shake with ice and strain into cocktail glass.

PRINCESS POUSSE CAFÉ

3/4 oz. Mr. Boston Apricot Flavored Brandy
1 1/2 tsp. Light Cream

Pour cream carefully on top of brandy, so that it does not mix. Use poussecafé glass.

PRINCETON COCKTAIL

1 oz. Mr. Boston Gin
1 oz. Dry Vermouth
Juice of 1/2 Lime

Stir with ice and strain into cocktail glass.

PUERTO APPLE

1 1/2 oz. Applejack
3/4 oz. Mr. Boston Rum
1 tbsp. Lime Juice
1 oz. Orgeat Syrup

Shake with ice and strain into old-fashioned glass over ice cubes. Decorate with a slice of lime.

PUNCHES

See Index on page 263 for complete list of Punch recipes.

PURPLE MASK

1 oz. Mr. Boston Vodka
1 oz. Grape Juice
1/2 oz. Mr. Boston Crème de Cacao (White)

Shake with ice and strain into cocktail glass.

PURPLE PASSION

1 1/2 oz. Mr. Boston Vodka
3 oz. Grapefruit Juice
3 oz. Grape Juice

Chill, stir, add sugar to taste, and serve in a Collins glass.

Q

QUAKER'S COCKTAIL
¾ oz.   Mr. Boston Rum
¾ oz.   Mr. Boston Five
     Star Brandy
Juice of ¼ Lemon
2 tsp.   Raspberry Syrup
Shake with ice and strain
into cocktail glass.

QUARTER DECK COCKTAIL
⅓ oz.   Balfour Cream
     Sherry
1½ oz. Mr. Boston Rum
Juice of ½ Lime
Stir with ice and strain into
cocktail glass.

QUEBEC
1½ oz. Mr. Boston Five
     Star Canadian Whisky
½ oz.   Dry Vermouth
1½ tsp. Amer Picon
1½ tsp. Maraschino
Shake with ice and strain
into cocktail glass rimmed
with sugar.

QUEEN BEE
1½ oz. Mr. Boston Lime
     Vodka
1 oz.   Mr. Boston
     Coffee Flavored Brandy
½ oz.   Balfour Cream
     Sherry
Shake with ice and strain
into cocktail glass.

QUEEN CHARLOTTE
2 oz.   Claret
1 oz.   Grenadine
Lemon Soda
Pour into collins glass over
ice cubes. Stir.

QUEEN ELIZABETH
1½ oz. Mr. Boston Gin
½ oz.   Dry Vermouth
1½ tsp. Benedictine
Stir with ice and strain into
cocktail glass.

Mandarine Mist

Mexican Coffee with whipped cream

R

RACQUET CLUB COCKTAIL

$1\frac{1}{2}$ oz. Mr. Boston Gin
$\frac{3}{4}$ oz. Dry Vermouth
1 dash Orange Bitters

Stir with ice and strain into cocktail glass.

RAMOS FIZZ

Juice of $\frac{1}{2}$ Lemon
1 Egg White
1 tsp. Powdered Sugar
2 oz. Mr. Boston Gin
1 tbsp. Light Cream
$\frac{1}{2}$ tsp. Mr. Boston Triple Sec

Shake with ice and strain into highball glass over two ice cubes. Fill with carbonated water and stir.

RATTLESNAKE COCKTAIL

$1\frac{1}{2}$ oz. Old Thompson Blended Whiskey
1 Egg White
1 tsp. Lemon Juice
$\frac{1}{2}$ tsp. Powdered Sugar
$\frac{1}{4}$ tsp. Absinthe Substitute

Shake with ice and strain into cocktail glass.

REBEL CHARGE

1 oz. Kentucky Tavern Bourbon
$\frac{1}{2}$ oz. Mr. Boston Triple Sec
1 tbsp. Orange Juice
1 tbsp. Lemon Juice
$\frac{1}{2}$ Egg White

Shake with ice and strain into old-fashioned glass over ice cubes. Add orange slice.

RED APPLE

1 oz. Mr. Boston 100 Proof Vodka
1 oz. Apple Juice
1 tbsp. Lemon Juice
1 tsp. Grenadine

Shake with ice and strain into cocktail glass.

RED CLOUD

$1\frac{1}{2}$ oz. Mr. Boston Gin
$\frac{1}{2}$ oz. Mr. Boston Apricot Flavored Brandy
1 tbsp. Lemon Juice
1 tsp. Grenadine

Shake with ice and strain into cocktail glass.

RED RAIDER

1 oz. Kentucky Tavern Bourbon
½ oz. Mr. Boston Triple Sec
1 oz. Lemon Juice
1 dash Grenadine

Shake with ice and strain into cocktail glass.

RED SWIZZLE

Make the same as Gin Swizzle (see page 90) and add one tablespoon of grenadine. If desired, rum, brandy, or whiskey may be substituted for the gin.

REFORM COCKTAIL

¾ oz. Dry Vermouth
1½ oz. Dry Sherry
1 dash Orange Bitters

Stir with ice and strain into cocktail glass. Serve with a cherry.

REMSEN COOLER

½ tsp. Powdered Sugar
Carbonated Water
2 oz. Mr. Boston Gin

Into collins glass, put powdered sugar and 2 oz. carbonated water. Stir. Add ice cubes and gin. Fill with carbonated water or ginger ale and stir again. Insert a spiral of orange or lemon peel (or both) and dangle end over rim of glass.

RENAISSANCE COCKTAIL

1½ oz. Mr. Boston Gin
½ oz. Dry Sherry
1 tbsp. Light Cream

Shake with ice and strain into cocktail glass. Sprinkle with nutmeg.

RESOLUTE COCKTAIL

Juice of ¼ Lemon
½ oz. Mr. Boston Apricot Flavored Brandy
1 oz. Mr. Boston Gin

Shake with ice and strain into cocktail glass.

RHINE WINE CUP

4 tsp. Powdered Sugar
6 oz. Carbonated Water
1 oz. Mr. Boston Triple Sec
2 oz. Mr. Boston Five Star Brandy
16 oz. Corbett Canyon Vineyard Rhine Wine

Mix ingredients and pour into large glass pitcher over cubes of ice. Stir and decorate with fruits in season. Insert rind of cucumber on each side of pitcher. Top with mint sprigs. Serve in claret glasses.

RICKEYS

See Index on page 264 for complete list of Rickey recipes.

Peppermint Freeze

ROAD RUNNER

1 oz. Mr. Boston Vodka
1/2 oz. Amaretto di Saronno
1/2 oz. Coconut Cream

Mix in blender with 1/2 scoop of crushed ice for 15 seconds. Rim edge of a chilled champagne glass with a slice of orange. Dip rim in a sugar and nutmeg mixture. Pour cocktail into the prepared glass. Top with a dash of nutmeg.

ROBERT E. LEE COOLER

Into collins glass, put:

Juice of 1/2 Lime
1/2 tsp. Powdered Sugar
2 oz. Carbonated Water

Stir. Add ice cubes and:

1/4 tsp. Absinthe Substitute
2 oz. Mr. Boston Dry Gin

Fill with ginger ale and stir again. Add a spiral of orange or lemon peel (or both) and dangle end over rim of glass.

ROBIN'S NEST

1 oz. Mr. Boston Vodka
1 oz. Cranberry Juice
1/2 oz. Mr. Boston Crème de Cacao (White)

Shake with ice and strain into cocktail glass.

ROB ROY

3/4 oz. Sweet Vermouth
1 1/2 oz. Desmond and Duff Scotch

Stir with ice and strain into cocktail glass.

ROBSON COCKTAIL

2 tsp. Lemon Juice
1 tbsp. Orange Juice
1 1/2 tsp. Grenadine
1 oz. Jamaica Rum

Shake with ice and strain into cocktail glass.

ROCK & RYE COCKTAIL

1 oz. Mr. Boston Rock & Rye
1 oz. White Port
1 1/2 tsp. Dry Vermouth

Stir with ice and strain into cocktail glass.

ROCK & RYE COOLER

1 oz. Mr. Boston Rock & Rye
1 1/2 oz. Mr. Boston Vodka
1 tbsp. Lime Juice
Bitter Lemon Soda

Shake with ice and strain into collins glass over ice.

ROCOCO

1 oz. Mr. Boston Cherry Vodka
1 oz. Orange Juice
1/2 oz. Mr. Boston Triple Sec

Shake with ice and strain into cocktail glass.

ROLLS-ROYCE
½ oz.   Dry Vermouth
½ oz.   Sweet Vermouth
1½ oz.   Mr. Boston Gin
¼ tsp.   Benedictine
Stir with ice and strain into
cocktail glass.

RORY O'MORE
¾ oz.   Sweet Vermouth
1½ oz.   Irish Whisky
1 dash   Orange Bitters
Stir with ice and strain into
cocktail glass.

ROSE COCKTAIL
(ENGLISH)
½ oz.   Mr. Boston
   Apricot Flavored
   Brandy
½ oz.   Dry Vermouth
1 oz.   Mr. Boston Gin
½ tsp.   Lemon Juice
1 tsp.   Grenadine
Moisten rim of cocktail
glass with lemon juice and
dip into powdered sugar.
Shake ingredients above
with ice and strain into
prepared glass.

ROSE COCKTAIL
(FRENCH)
½ oz.   Mr. Boston
   Cherry Flavored
   Brandy
½ oz.   Dry Vermouth
1½ oz.   Mr. Boston Gin
Stir with ice and strain into
cocktail glass.

ROSELYN COCKTAIL
¾ oz.   Dry Vermouth
1½ oz.   Mr. Boston Gin
½ tsp.   Grenadine
Stir with ice and strain into
cocktail glass. Add a twist of
lemon peel.

ROSITA
1 oz.   Gavilan Tequila
½ oz.   Dry Vermouth
½ oz.   Sweet Vermouth
1 oz.   Campari
Stir in old-fashioned glass
with cracked ice. Add a
twist of lemon peel and
serve with short straws.

ROYAL CLOVER CLUB
COCKTAIL
Juice of 1 Lime
1 tbsp.   Grenadine
1 Egg Yolk
1½ oz.   Mr. Boston Gin
Shake with ice and strain
into flip glass.

ROYAL COCKTAIL
1 Whole Egg
Juice of ½ Lemon
½ tsp.   Powdered Sugar
1½ oz.   Mr. Boston Gin
Shake with ice and strain
into flip glass.

ROYAL GIN FIZZ
Juice of ½ Lemon
1 tsp.   Powdered Sugar
2 oz.   Mr. Boston Gin
1 Whole Egg
Shake with ice and strain
into highball glass with two
ice cubes. Fill with
carbonated water and stir.

ROYAL PURPLE PUNCH

Pour two bottles (750ml size) claret and two large bottles ginger ale over ice cubes in punch bowl. Stir well. Float thin slices of lemon studded with cloves on top. Serve in punch glasses.

ROYAL SMILE COCKTAIL

Juice of ¼ Lemon
1 tsp.   Grenadine
½ oz.   Mr. Boston Gin
1 oz.   Mr. Boston Apple Brandy

Stir with ice and strain into cocktail glass.

RUBY FIZZ

Juice of ½ Lemon
1 tsp.   Powdered Sugar
1 Egg White
1 tsp.   Grenadine
2 oz.   Mr. Boston Sloe Gin

Shake with ice and strain into highball glass over two ice cubes. Fill with carbonated water and stir.

RUM COBBLER

In a goblet, dissolve 1 teaspoon powdered sugar in 2 oz. carbonated water. Fill goblet with shaved ice, and add **2 oz. Mr. Boston Rum**. Stir and decorate with fruits in season. Serve with a straw.

RUM COLA

See Cuba Libra recipe on page 69.

RUM COLLINS

Juice of 1 Lime
1 tsp.   Powdered Sugar
2 oz.   Mr. Boston Rum

Shake with ice and strain into collins glass. Add several ice cubes, fill with carbonated water, and stir. Decorate with a slice of lemon and a cherry. Serve with a straw.

RUM COOLER

In collins glass, dissolve ½ teaspoon powdered sugar in 2 oz. carbonated water. Stir. Fill glass with ice and add **2 oz. Mr. Boston Rum**. Fill with carbonated water or ginger ale and stir again. Insert a spiral of orange or lemon peel (or both) and dangle end over rim of glass.

RUM DAISY

Juice of ½ Lemon
½ tsp.   Powdered Sugar
1 tsp.   Grenadine
2 oz.   Mr. Boston Rum

Shake with ice and strain into stein or metal cup. Add one ice cube and decorate with fruit.

RUM DUBONNET®

1½ oz.   Mr. Boston Rum
1½ tsp. Dubonnet®
1 tsp.   Lemon Juice

Shake with ice and strain into cocktail glass.

RUM EGGNOG

1 Whole Egg
1 tsp. Powdered Sugar
2 oz. Mr. Boston Rum
6 oz. Milk

Shake with ice and strain into collins glass. Sprinkle nutmeg on top.

RUM FIX

Juice of 1/2 Lemon or 1 Lime
1 tsp. Powdered Sugar
1 tsp. Water

Stir together in a highball glass and fill glass with ice. Add 2 1/2 oz. Mr. Boston Rum. Stir and add slice of lemon. Serve with a straw.

RUM HIGHBALL

Pour 2 oz. Mr. Boston Rum in highball glass over ice cubes and fill with ginger ale or carbonated water. Add a twist of lemon peel, if desired, and stir.

RUM OLD FASHIONED

1/2 tsp. Powdered Sugar
1 dash Bitters
1 tsp. Water
1 1/2 oz. Mr. Boston Rum
1 tsp. 151 Proof Rum

Stir sugar, bitters, and water in old-fashioned glass. When sugar is dissolved, add ice cubes and light rum. Add a twist of lime peel and float the 151-proof rum on top.

RUM MARTINI

4 to 5 parts Mr. Boston Rum
Dash Dry Vermouth

Serve on the rocks with a twist of lemon.

RUM MILK PUNCH

1 tsp. Powdered Sugar
2 oz. Mr. Boston Rum
1 cup Milk

Shake with ice, strain into collins glass and sprinkle nutmeg on top.

RUM RICKEY

Juice of 1/2 Lime
1 1/2 oz. Mr. Boston Rum

Pour into highball glass over ice cubes and fill with carbonated water and ice cubes. Stir. Add a wedge of lime.

RUM RUNNER

1 1/2 oz. Mr. Boston Gin
Juice of 1 Lime
1 oz. Pineapple Juice
1 tsp. Sugar
1 dash Bitters

Shake with ice and strain over ice cubes in an old-fashioned glass rimmed with salt.

RUM SCREWDRIVER

1 1/2 oz. Mr. Boston Rum
5 oz. Orange Juice

Combine ingredients in highball glass with ice cubes.

RUM SOUR

Juice of $1/2$ Lemon
$1/2$ tsp. Powdered Sugar
2 oz. Mr. Boston Rum

Shake with ice and strain into sour glass. Decorate with a half-slice of lemon and a cherry.

RUM SWIZZLE

Made same as Gin Swizzle (see page 90) substituting 2 oz. Mr. Boston Rum for gin.

RUM TODDY

In old-fashioned glass dissolve $1/2$ teaspoon powdered sugar in 2 teaspoons water. Stir and add 2 oz. Mr. Boston Rum and a cube of ice. Stir again and add a twist of lemon peel.

RUM TODDY (HOT)

Put lump of sugar into hot whiskey glass and fill $2/3$ with boiling water. Add 2 oz. Mr. Boston Rum. Stir and decorate with a slice of lemon. Sprinkle nutmeg on top.

RUSSIAN BEAR COCKTAIL

1 oz. Mr. Boston Vodka
$1/2$ oz. Mr. Boston Crème de Cacao (White)
1 tbsp. Light Cream

Stir with ice and strain into cocktail glass.

RUSSIAN COCKTAIL

$3/4$ oz. Mr. Boston Crème de Cacao (White)
$3/4$ oz. Mr. Boston Gin
$3/4$ oz. Mr. Boston Vodka

Shake with ice and strain into cocktail glass.

RUSTY NAIL

$3/4$ oz. Desmond & Duff Scotch
$1/4$ oz. Drambuie

Serve in old-fashioned glass with ice cubes. Float Drambuie on top.

RYE HIGHBALL

Put 2 oz. Rye Whiskey in highball glass over ice cubes and fill with ginger ale or carbonated water and ice cubes. Add a twist of lemon peel, if desired, and stir.

RYE WHISKEY COCKTAIL

1 dash Bitters
1 tsp. Powdered Sugar
2 oz. Rye Whiskey

Shake with ice and strain into cocktail glass. Serve with a cherry.

S

ST. CHARLES PUNCH
1 oz.   Mr. Boston Five Star Brandy
½ oz.   Mr. Boston Triple Sec
3 oz.   Port
Juice of 1 Lemon
1 tsp.   Sugar
Shake all ingredients with ice except port. Strain into collins glass with ice. Top with port. Add a slice of lemon and a cherry.

ST. PATRICK'S DAY
¾ oz.   Mr. Boston Crème de Menthe (Green)
¾ oz.   Chartreuse (Green)
¾ oz.   Irish Whisky
1 dash   Bitters
Stir with ice and strain into cocktail glass.

SAKE MARTINI (SAKINI)
1 part Sake
3 parts Mr. Boston Gin
Stir with ice, strain into 3- or 4-oz. cocktail glass and serve with an olive.

SALTY DOG
1½ oz.   Mr. Boston Gin
5 oz.   Grapefruit Juice
¼ tsp.   Salt
Pour into highball glass over ice cubes. Stir well. (**Mr. Boston Vodka** may be substituted for the **Mr. Boston Gin**.)

SAND-MARTIN COCKTAIL
1 tsp.   Chartreuse (Green)
1½ oz.   Sweet Vermouth
1½ oz.   Mr. Boston Gin
Stir with ice and strain into cocktail glass.

SAN FRANCISCO COCKTAIL
¾ oz.   Mr. Boston Sloe Gin
¾ oz.   Sweet Vermouth
¾ oz.   Dry Vermouth
1 dash   Bitters
1 dash   Orange Bitters
Shake with ice and strain into cocktail glass. Serve with a cherry.

SANGAREES
See Index on page 265 for complete list of Sangaree recipes.

SANGRIA

1/4 cup Sugar (or to taste)
1 cup Water
1 Thinly Sliced Orange
1 Thinly Sliced Lime
1 750ml bottle Corbett
    Canyon Vineyard Red
    or Rosé Wine
6 oz. Sparkling Water
Other fruit as desired (i.e.
    bananas, strawberry).

Dissolve sugar in water in large pitcher. Add fruit and wine and 12 or more ice cubes. Stir until cold. Add sparkling water. Serve, putting some fruit in each glass.

SAN SEBASTIAN

1 oz.   Mr. Boston Gin
1 1/2 tsp. Mr. Boston Rum
1 tbsp.   Grapefruit Juice
1 1/2 tsp. Mr. Boston Triple
            Sec
1 tbsp.   Lemon Juice

Shake with ice and strain into cocktail glass.

SANTIAGO COCKTAIL

1/2 tsp.   Powdered Sugar
1/4 tsp.   Grenadine
Juice of 1 Lime
1 1/2 oz. Mr. Boston Rum

Shake with ice and strain into cocktail glass.

SANTINI'S POUSSE CAFÉ

1/2 oz.   Mr. Boston Five
            Star Brandy
1 tbsp.   Maraschino
1/2 oz.   Mr. Boston Triple
            Sec
1/2 oz.   Mr. Boston Rum

Pour in order given into pousse-café glass.

SARATOGA COCKTAIL

2 oz.   Mr. Boston Five
            Star Brandy
2 dashes Bitters
1 tsp.   Lemon Juice
1 tsp.   Pineapple Juice
1/2 tsp. Maraschino

Shake with ice and strain into cocktail glass.

SARONNO

1 oz.   Amaretto di
            Saronno
1 oz.   Mr. Boston Five
            Star Brandy
1 oz.   Light Cream

Shake well with cracked ice. Strain and serve in cocktail glass.

SARONNO COLADA (NUTTY COLADA)

3 oz.   Amaretto di
            Saronno
3 tbsp.   Coconut Milk
3 tbsp.   Crushed
            Pineapple

Put in an electric blender with 2 cups of crushed ice and blend at high speed for a short time. Pour into a collins glass and serve with a straw.

SARONNO MIST

1 1/2 oz. Amaretto di
            Saronno

Serve in an old-fashioned glass over crushed ice with a twist of lemon or a wedge of lime, if desired.

SARONNO ROSE

1½ oz. Amaretto di Saronno
½ oz. Roses Lime Juice
Club Soda

Pour Amaretto di Saronno and lime juice over ice in a collins glass and fill with club soda.

SAUCY SUE COCKTAIL

½ tsp. Mr. Boston Apricot Flavored Brandy
½ tsp. Absinthe Substitute
2 oz. Mr. Boston Apple Brandy

Stir with ice and strain into cocktail glass.

SAUTERNE CUP

4 tsp. Powdered Sugar
6 oz. Carbonated Water
1 tbsp. Mr. Boston Triple Sec
1 tbsp. Curaçao
2 oz. Mr. Boston Five Star Brandy
16 oz. Sauterne

Put all ingredients in a large glass pitcher with ice. Stir and decorate with fruits in season and also rind of cucumber inserted on each side of pitcher. Top with a small bunch of mint sprigs. Serve in claret glass.

SAVANNAH

Juice of ½ Orange
1 oz. Mr. Boston Gin
1 dash Mr. Boston Crème de Cacao (White)
1 Egg White

Shake with ice and strain into cocktail glass.

SAXON COCKTAIL

Juice of ½ Lime
½ tsp. Grenadine
1¾ oz. Mr. Boston Rum

Shake with ice and strain into cocktail glass. Serve with a twist of orange peel.

SAZERAC

½ tsp. Pernod
1½ oz. Kentucky Tavern Bourbon
2 tsp. Sugar Syrup
3 dashes Bitters

In an old-fashioned glass, swirl Pernod until inside of glass is completely coated. Mix remaining ingredients in cocktail shaker and strain into coated glass. Add a twist of lemon.

SCOOTER

1 oz. Amaretto di Saronno
1 oz. Mr. Boston Five Star Brandy
1 oz. Light Cream

Combine in an electric blender or shake well with cracked ice. Strain into cocktail glass.

SCOTCH BIRD FLYER

1½ oz. Desmond & Duff Scotch
1 Egg Yolk
½ oz. Mr. Boston Triple Sec
½ tsp. Powdered Sugar
1 oz. Light Cream

Shake with ice and strain into champagne glass.

SCOTCH BISHOP COCKTAIL

1 oz. Desmond & Duff Scotch
1 tbsp. Orange Juice
½ oz. Dry Vermouth
½ tsp. Mr. Boston Triple Sec
¼ tsp. Powdered Sugar

Shake with ice and strain into cocktail glass. Add a twist of lemon peel.

SCOTCH COOLER

2 oz. Desmond & Duff Scotch
3 dashes Mr. Boston Crème de Menthe (White)

Pour into highball glass over ice cubes. Fill with chilled carbonated water and stir.

SCOTCH HIGHBALL

Put 2 oz. Desmond & Duff Scotch in highball glass with ice cubes and fill with ginger ale or carbonated water. Add a twist of lemon peel, if desired, and stir.

SCOTCH HOLIDAY SOUR

1½ oz. Desmond & Duff Scotch
1 oz. Mr. Boston Cherry Flavored Brandy
½ oz. Sweet Vermouth
1 oz. Lemon Juice

Shake with ice and strain into old-fashioned glass over ice cubes. Add a slice of lemon.

SCOTCH MILK PUNCH

2 oz. Desmond & Duff Scotch
6 oz. Milk
1 tsp. Powdered Sugar

Shake with ice and strain into collins glass. Sprinkle with nutmeg.

SCOTCH MIST

Pack old-fashioned glass with crushed ice. Pour in 2 oz. Desmond & Duff Scotch. Add a twist of lemon peel. Serve with short straw.

SCOTCH OLD FASHIONED

Make same as Old Fashioned (see page 131), but substitute Desmond & Duff Scotch.

SCOTCH RICKEY

Juice of ½ Lime
1½ oz. Desmond & Duff Scotch

Pour into highball glass over ice and fill with carbonated water. Add a rind of lime. Stir.

SCOTCH-SOUR

$1^1/_2$ oz. Desmond & Duff
  Scotch
Juice of $^1/_2$ Lime
$^1/_2$ tsp. Powdered Sugar
Shake with ice and strain
into sour glass. Decorate
with a half-slice of lemon
and a cherry.

SCOTCH STINGER

Make same as Stinger
Cocktail on page 165, but
substitute **Desmond & Duff
Scotch** for brandy.

SCREWDRIVER

Put two or three cubes of
ice into highball glass. Add
2 oz. **Mr. Boston Vodka.**
Fill balance of glass with
orange juice and stir.

SEABOARD

1 oz.   Old Thompson
  Blended Whiskey
1 oz.   Mr. Boston Gin
1 tbsp. Lemon Juice
1 tsp.   Powdered Sugar
Shake with ice and strain
into old-fashioned glass
over ice cubes. Decorate
with mint leaves.

SENSATION COCKTAIL

Juice of $^1/_4$ Lemon
$1^1/_2$ oz. Mr. Boston Gin
1 tsp.   Maraschino
Shake with ice and strain
into cocktail glass. Add two
sprigs of fresh mint.

SEPTEMBER MORN COCKTAIL

1 Egg White
$1^1/_2$ oz. Mr. Boston Rum
Juice of $^1/_2$ Lime
1 tsp.   Grenadine
Shake with ice and strain
into cocktail glass.

SEVENTH HEAVEN COCKTAIL

2 tsp.   Grapefruit Juice
1 tbsp. Maraschino
$1^1/_2$ oz. Mr. Boston Gin
Shake with ice and strain
into cocktail glass. Decorate
with a sprig of fresh mint.

SEVILLA COCKTAIL

$^1/_2$ tsp. Powdered Sugar
1 Whole Egg
1 oz.   Port
1 oz.   Mr. Boston Rum
Shake with ice and strain
into flip glass.

SHADY GROVE

$1^1/_2$ oz. Mr. Boston Gin
Juice of $^1/_2$ Lemon
1 tsp.   Powdered Sugar
Shake with ice and strain
into highball glass with ice
cubes. Fill with ginger
beer.

SHALOM

$1^1/_2$ oz. Mr. Boston 100
  Proof Vodka
1 oz.   Madeira
1 tbsp. Orange Juice
Shake with ice and strain
into old-fashioned glass
over ice cubes. Add an
orange slice.

SHAMROCK
1¹/₂ oz. Irish Whisky
¹/₂ oz. Dry Vermouth
1 tsp. Mr. Boston Creme de Menthe (Green)

Stir with ice and strain into cocktail glass. Serve with an olive.

SHANDY GAFF
5 oz. Beer
5 oz. Ginger Ale

Pour into collins glass and stir.

SHANGHAI COCKTAIL
Juice of ¹/₄ Lemon
1 tsp Mr. Boston Anisette
1 oz. Jamaica Rum
¹/₂ tsp. Grenadine

Shake with ice and strain into cocktail glass.

SHAVETAIL
1¹/₂ oz. Mr. Boston Peppermint Schnapps
1 oz. Pineapple Juice
1 oz. Light Cream

Shake with ice and strain into old-fashioned glass.

SHERRY-and-EGG COCKTAIL
Place an egg in a cocktail glass, being careful not to break the yolk. Fill glass with Balfour Cream Sherry.

SHERRY COBBLER
1 tsp. Powdered Sugar
2 oz. Carbonated Water
2 oz. Sweet Sherry

In a goblet dissolve powdered sugar in carbonated water. Fill goblet with ice and add sherry. Stir and decorate with fruits in season. Serve with straws.

SHERRY COCKTAIL
2¹/₂ oz. Balfour Cream Sherry
1 dash Bitters

Stir with ice and strain into cocktail glass. Add a twist of orange peel.

SHERRY EGGNOG
1 Whole Egg
1 tsp. Powdered Sugar
2 oz. Balfour Cream Sherry
Milk

Shake above ingredients, except milk, with ice and strain into collins glass. Fill glass with milk and stir. Sprinkle nutmeg on top.

SHERRY FLIP
1 Whole Egg
1 tsp. Powdered Sugar
1¹/₂ oz. Balfour Cream Sherry
2 tsp. Light Cream (if desired)

Shake with ice and strain into flip glass. Sprinkle a little nutmeg on top.

SHERRY MILK PUNCH
1 tsp. Powdered Sugar
2 oz. Balfour Cream Sherry
16 oz. Milk
Shake with ice, strain into collins glass, and sprinkle nutmeg on top.

SHERRY SANGAREE
1/2 tsp. Powdered Sugar
1 tsp. Water
2 oz. Balfour Cream Sherry
Splash Carbonated Water
1 tbsp. Port
In an old-fashioned glass dissolve powdered sugar in water, add sherry and stir. Add ice cubes and a splash of carbonated water, leaving enough room on which to float port. Add port. Sprinkle lightly with nutmeg.

SHERRY TWIST COCKTAIL
1 oz. Balfour Cream Sherry
1/2 oz. Mr. Boston Five Star Brandy
1/2 oz. Dry Vermouth
1/2 oz. Mr. Boston Triple Sec
1/2 tsp. Lemon Juice
Shake with ice and strain into cocktail glass. Top with pinch of cinnamon and a twist of orange peel.

SHRINER COCKTAIL
1 1/2 oz. Mr. Boston Five Star Brandy
1 1/2 oz. Mr. Boston Sloe Gin
2 dashes Bitters
1/2 tsp. Sugar Syrup
Stir with ice and strain into cocktail glass. Add a twist of lemon peel.

SIDECAR COCKTAIL
Juice of 1/4 Lemon
1/2 oz. Mr. Boston Triple Sec
1 oz. Mr. Boston Five Star Brandy
Shake with ice and strain into cocktail glass.

SILVER BULLET
1 oz. Mr. Boston Gin
1 oz. Kümmel
1 tbsp. Lemon Juice
Shake with ice and strain into cocktail glass.

SILVER COCKTAIL
1 oz. Dry Vermouth
1 oz. Mr. Boston Gin
2 dashes Orange Bitters
1/4 tsp. Sugar Syrup
1/2 tsp. Maraschino
Stir with ice and strain into cocktail glass. Add a twist of lemon peel.

SILVER FIZZ
Juice of 1/2 Lemon
1 tsp. Powdered Sugar
2 oz. Mr. Boston Gin
1 Egg White
Carbonated Water
Shake with ice and strain
into highball glass over two
ice cubes.

SILVER KING COCKTAIL
1 Egg White
Juice of 1/4 Lemon
1 1/2 oz. Mr. Boston Gin
1/2 tsp. Powdered Sugar
2 dashes Orange Bitters
Shake with ice and strain
into cocktail glass.

SILVER STALLION FIZZ
1 scoop Vanilla Ice
Cream
2 oz. Mr. Boston Gin
Carbonated Water
Shake gin and ice cream
with ice and strain into
highball glass. Fill with
carbonated water and stir.

SILVER STREAK
1 1/2 oz. Mr. Boston Gin
1 oz. Kümmel
Shake with ice and strain
into cocktail glass.

SINGAPORE SLING
Juice of 1/2 Lemon
1 tsp. Powdered Sugar
2 oz. Mr. Boston Gin
Carbonated Water
1/2 oz. Mr. Boston
Cherry Flavored
Brandy
Shake lemon, sugar, and
gin with ice and strain into
collins glass. Add ice cubes
and fill with carbonated
water. Float cherry flavored
brandy on top. Decorate
with fruits in season and
serve with straws.

SIR WALTER COCKTAIL
3/4 oz. Mr. Boston Rum
3/4 oz. Mr. Boston Five
Star Brandy
1 tsp. Grenadine
1 tsp. Mr. Boston Triple
Sec
1 tsp. Lemon Juice
Shake with ice and strain
into cocktail glass.

SLINGS
See Index on page 265 for
complete list of Sling
recipes.

SLOEBERRY COCKTAIL
1 dash Bitters
2 oz. Mr. Boston Sloe
Gin
Stir with ice and strain into
cocktail glass.

SLOE DRIVER
Put two or three ice cubes into highball glass and add 2 oz. Mr. Boston Sloe Gin. Fill with orange juice and stir.

SLOE GIN COCKTAIL
2 oz.   Mr. Boston Sloe Gin
1 dash   Orange Bitters
$1/4$ tsp.   Dry Vermouth
Stir with ice and strain into cocktail glass.

SLOE GIN COLLINS
Juice of $1/2$ Lemon
2 oz.   Mr. Boston Sloe Gin
Carbonated Water
Shake lemon and sloe gin with ice and strain into collins glass. Add several ice cubes, fill with carbonated water and stir. Decorate with slices of lemon, orange, and a cherry. Serve with straws.

SLOE GIN FIZZ
Juice of $1/2$ Lemon
1 tsp.   Powdered Sugar
2 oz.   Mr. Boston Sloe Gin
Shake with ice and strain into highball glass with two ice cubes. Fill with carbonated water and stir. Decorate with a slice of lemon.

SLOE GIN FLIP
1 Whole Egg
1 tsp.   Powdered Sugar
1 tbsp.   Mr. Boston Sloe Gin
2 tsp.   Light Cream (if desired)
Shake with ice and strain into flip glass. Sprinkle a little nutmeg on top.

SLOE GIN RICKEY
Juice of $1/2$ Lime
2 oz.   Mr. Boston Sloe Gin
Carbonated Water
Pour into highball glass over ice cubes. Stir. Drop a lime rind into glass.

SLOE TEQUILA
1 oz.   Gavilan Tequila
$1/2$ oz.   Mr. Boston Sloe Gin
1 tbsp.   Lime Juice
Combine ingredients with a half-cup of crushed ice in an electric blender. Blend at low speed and pour into old-fashioned glass. Add ice cubes and cucumber peel.

SLOE VERMOUTH
1 oz.   Mr. Boston Sloe Gin
1 oz.   Dry Vermouth
1 tbsp.   Lemon Juice
Shake with ice and strain into cocktail glass.

SLOPPY JOE'S COCKTAIL NO. 1
Juice of 1 Lime
1/4 tsp. Mr. Boston Triple Sec
1/4 tsp. Grenadine
3/4 oz. Mr. Boston Rum
3/4 oz. Dry Vermouth
Shake with ice and strain into cocktail glass.

SLOPPY JOE'S COCKTAIL NO. 2
3/4 oz. Pineapple Juice
3/4 oz. Mr. Boston Five Star Brandy
3/4 oz. Port
1/4 tsp. Mr. Boston Triple Sec
1/4 tsp. Grenadine
Shake with ice and strain into cocktail glass.

SMASHES
See Index on page 266 for complete list of Smash recipes.

SMILE COCKTAIL
1 oz. Grenadine
1 oz. Mr. Boston Gin
1/2 tsp. Lemon Juice
Shake with ice and strain into cocktail glass.

SMILER COCKTAIL
1/2 oz. Sweet Vermouth
1/2 oz. Dry Vermouth
1 oz. Mr. Boston Gin
1 dash Bitters
1/4 tsp. Orange Juice
Shake with ice and strain into cocktail glass.

SNOWBALL
1 1/2 oz. Mr. Boston Gin
1/2 oz. Mr. Boston Anisette
1 tbsp. Light Cream
Shake with ice and strain into cocktail glass.

SNYDER
1 1/2 oz. Mr. Boston Gin
1/2 oz. Dry Vermouth
1/2 oz. Mr. Boston Triple Sec
Shake with ice and strain into cocktail glass. Add a twist of lemon peel.

SOCIETY COCKTAIL
1 1/2 oz. Mr. Boston Gin
3/4 oz. Dry Vermouth
1/4 tsp. Grenadine
Stir with ice and strain into cocktail glass.

SOMBRERO
1 1/2 oz. Mr. Boston Coffee Flavored Brandy
1 oz. Light Cream
Pour brandy into old-fashioned glass over ice cubes. Float cream on top.

SOOTHER COCKTAIL
1/2 oz. Mr. Boston Five Star Brandy
1/2 oz. Mr. Boston Apple Brandy
1/2 oz. Mr. Boston Triple Sec
Juice of 1/2 Lemon
1 tsp. Powdered Sugar
Shake with ice and strain into cocktail glass.

SOUL KISS COCKTAIL
1 1/2 tsp. Orange Juice
1 1/2 tsp. Dubonnet®
3/4 oz. Dry Vermouth
3/4 oz. Kentucky Tavern Bourbon
Shake with ice and strain into cocktail glass.

SOURS
See Index on page 266 for complete list of Sour recipes.

SOUTHERN BRIDE
1 1/2 oz. Mr. Boston Gin
1 oz. Grapefruit Juice
1 dash Maraschino
Shake with ice and strain into cocktail glass.

SOUTHERN GIN COCKTAIL
2 oz. Mr. Boston Gin
2 dashes Orange Bitters
1/2 tsp. Mr. Boston Triple Sec
Stir with ice and strain into cocktail glass. Add a twist of lemon peel.

SOUTH OF THE BORDER
1 oz. Gavilan Tequila
3/4 oz. Mr. Boston Coffee Flavored Brandy
Juice of 1/2 Lime
Shake with ice and strain into sour glass. Add a lime slice.

SOUTH-SIDE COCKTAIL
Juice of 1/2 Lemon
1 tsp. Powdered Sugar
1 1/2 oz. Mr. Boston Gin
Shake with ice and strain into cocktail glass. Add two sprigs of fresh mint.

SOUTH-SIDE FIZZ
Juice of 1/2 Lemon
1 tsp Powdered Sugar
2 oz. Mr. Boston Gin
Shake with ice and strain into highball glass with ice cubes. Fill with carbonated water and stir. Add fresh mint leaves.

SOVIET
1 1/2 oz. Mr. Boston Vodka
1/2 oz. Amontillado Sherry
1/2 oz. Dry Vermouth
Shake with ice and strain into old-fashioned glass over ice cubes. Add a twist of lemon peel.

SPANISH COFFEE
1 oz. Felipe II Spanish Brandy
Hot Coffee
Add coffee to brandy in a mug and top with whipped cream.

SPANISH TOWN COCKTAIL
2 oz. Mr. Boston Rum
1 tsp. Mr. Boston Triple Sec
Stir with ice and strain into cocktail glass.

SPECIAL ROUGH COCKTAIL

1 1/2 oz. Mr. Boston Apple Brandy
1 1/2 oz. Mr. Boston Five Star Brandy
1/2 tsp. Absinthe Substitute

Stir with ice and strain into cocktail glass.

SPENCER COCKTAIL

3/4 oz. Mr. Boston Apricot Flavored Brandy
1 1/2 oz. Mr. Boston Gin
1 dash Bitters
1/4 tsp. Orange Juice

Shake with ice and strain into cocktail glass. Add a cherry and twist of orange peel.

SPHINX COCKTAIL

1 1/2 oz. Mr. Boston Gin
1 1/2 tsp. Sweet Vermouth
1 1/2 tsp. Dry Vermouth

Stir with ice and strain into cocktail glass. Serve with a slice of lemon.

SPRING FEELING COCKTAIL

1 tbsp. Lemon Juice
1/2 oz. Chartreuse (Green)
1 oz. Mr. Boston Gin

Shake with ice and strain into cocktail glass.

SPRITZER

Pour 3 oz. chilled Valley Ridge white wine into highball glass or wine glass with ice cubes. Fill balance with carbonated water and stir gently.

STANLEY COCKTAIL

Juice of 1/4 Lemon
1 tsp. Grenadine
3/4 oz. Mr. Boston Gin
1/4 oz. Mr. Boston Rum

Shake with ice and strain into cocktail glass.

STAR COCKTAIL

1 oz. Mr. Boston Apple Brandy
1 oz. Sweet Vermouth
1 dash Bitters

Stir with ice and strain into cocktail glass. Add a twist of lemon peel.

STAR DAISY

Juice of 1/2 Lemon
1/2 tsp. Powdered Sugar
1 tsp. Grenadine
1 oz. Mr. Boston Gin
1 oz. Mr. Boston Apple Brandy

Shake with ice and strain into stein or metal cup. Add an ice cube and decorate with fruit.

STARS AND STRIPES
- 1/3 Grenadine
- 1/3 Heavy Cream
- 1/3 Blue Curaçao

Pour carefully, in order given, into pousse-café glass, so that each ingredient floats on preceding one.

STILETTO
- Juice of 1/2 Lemon
- 1 1/2 tsp. Amaretto di Saronno
- 1 1/2 oz. Kentucky Tavern Bourbon or Old Thompson Blended Whiskey

Pour into an old-fashioned glass over ice cubes and stir.

STINGER
- 1/2 oz. Mr. Boston Crème de Menthe (White)
- 1 1/2 oz. Mr. Boston Five Star Brandy

Shake with ice and strain into cocktail glass.

STIRRUP CUP
- 1 oz. Mr. Boston Cherry Flavored Brandy
- 1 oz. Mr. Boston Five Star Brandy
- Juice of 1/2 Lemon
- 1 tsp. Sugar

Shake with ice and strain into old-fashioned glass over ice cubes.

STONE COCKTAIL
- 1/2 oz. Mr. Boston Rum
- 1/2 oz. Sweet Vermouth
- 1 oz. Dry Sherry

Stir with ice and strain into cocktail glass.

STONE FENCE
- 2 dashes Bitters
- 2 oz. Desmond & Duff Scotch
- Carbonated Water or Cider

Fill highball glass with ice cubes. Add scotch and bitters and fill with carbonated water or cider. Stir.

STRAIGHT LAW COCKTAIL
- 3/4 oz. Mr. Boston Gin
- 1 1/2 oz. Dry Sherry

Stir with ice and strain into cocktail glass.

STRAWBERRIES AND CREAM
- 1 oz. Mr. Boston Original Strawberry Schnapps
- 1 1/2 tbsp. Sugar
- 2 oz. Half-and-Half
- 2 Whole Strawberries

Place in an electric blender with 2 cups of crushed ice and blend at high speed. Add 2 whole strawberries and blend for 10 seconds. Pour in a parfait glass and serve with a straw. Garnish with a fresh strawberry.

STRAWBERRY DAIQUIRI
1 oz.   Mr. Boston Rum
1/2 oz. Mr. Boston
         Original Strawberry
         Schnapps
1 oz.   Lime Juice
1 tsp.   Powdered Sugar
1 oz.   Fresh or Frozen
         Strawberries
Shake with ice and strain
into cocktail glass.

STRAWBERRY FIELDS FOREVER
2 oz.   Mr. Boston
         Original Strawberry
         Schnapps
1/2 oz. Mr. Boston Five
         Star Brandy
Pour over ice in a highball
glass. Fill with carbonated
water. Garnish with a fresh
strawberry.

STRAWBERRY MARGARITA
1 oz.   Gavilan Tequila
1/2 oz. Mr. Boston Triple
         Sec
1/2 oz. Mr. Boston
         Original Strawberry
         Schnapps
1 oz.   Lemon or Lime
         Juice
1 oz.   Fresh or Frozen
         Strawberries
If desired, rub rim of
cocktail glass with a rind of
lemon or lime, dip rim in
salt. Shake ingredients with
ice and strain into the glass.

STRAWBERRY SUNRISE
2 oz.   Mr. Boston
         Original Strawberry
         Schnapps
1/2 oz. Grenadine Syrup
Pour over ice in a highball
glass. Fill with orange juice.
Garnish with a fresh
strawberry.

SUISSESSE COCKTAIL
2 oz.   Mr. Boston
         Anisette
1 Egg White
Shake with ice and strain
into cocktail glass.

SUNSHINE COCKTAIL
3/4 oz. Sweet Vermouth
1 1/2 oz. Mr. Boston Gin
1 dash   Bitters
Stir with ice and strain into
cocktail glass. Add a twist of
orange peel.

SUSIE TAYLOR
Juice of 1/2 Lime
2 oz.   Mr. Boston Rum
Pour into collins glass over
ice cubes and fill with
ginger ale. Stir.

SWEET MARIA
1 tbsp. Light Cream
1/2 oz. Amaretto di
         Saronno
1 oz.   Mr. Boston Vodka
Shake with cracked ice.
Strain into cocktail glass.

SWEET PATOOTIE COCKTAIL

1 oz.   Mr. Boston Gin
½ oz.   Mr. Boston Triple Sec
1 tbsp. Orange Juice

Shake with ice and strain into cocktail glass.

SWISS FAMILY COCKTAIL

½ tsp. Absinthe Substitute
2 dashes Bitters
¾ oz. Dry Vermouth
1½ oz. Old Thompson Blended Whiskey

Stir with ice and strain into cocktail glass.

SWIZZLES

See Index on page 266 for complete list of Swizzle recipes.

T

TAHITI CLUB
2 oz.   Mr. Boston Rum
1 tbsp. Lemon Juice
1 tbsp. Lime Juice
1 tbsp. Pineapple Juice
1/2 tsp. Maraschino
Shake with ice and strain into old-fashioned glass over ice cubes. Add a slice of lemon.

TAILSPIN COCKTAIL
3/4 oz. Mr. Boston Gin
3/4 oz. Sweet Vermouth
3/4 oz. Chartreuse (Green)
1 dash Orange Bitters
Stir with ice and strain into cocktail glass. Add a twist of lemon peel and a cherry or olive.

TANGO COCKTAIL
1 tbsp. Orange Juice
1/2 oz. Dry Vermouth
1/2 oz. Sweet Vermouth
1 oz.   Mr. Boston Gin
1/2 tsp. Mr. Boston Triple Sec
Shake with ice and strain into a cocktail glass.

TCHOUPITOLAS STREET GUZZLE
1 oz.   Mr. Boston Rum
Ginger Beer
Pour rum into highball glass over ice cubes. Add ginger beer.

TEA SARONNO
6 oz.   Hot Tea
1 1/2 to 2 oz. Amaretto di Saronno
Whipped Cream
Pour hot tea into a stemmed glass, using a spoon in glass to prevent cracking. Add Amaretto di Saronno but do not stir. Top with chilled whipped cream.

TEMPTATION COCKTAIL
1 1/2 oz. Old Thompson Blended Whiskey
1/2 tsp. Mr. Boston Triple Sec
1/2 tsp. Absinthe Substitute
1/2 tsp. Dubonnet®
Shake with ice and strain into cocktail glass. Add twists of lemon and orange peel.

Tequila Mockingbird

TEMPTER COCKTAIL
1 oz. Port
1 oz. Mr. Boston
      Apricot Flavored
      Brandy
Stir with ice and strain into cocktail glass.

TEQUILA COLLINS
Make same as Tom Collins (see page 174) but use Gavilan Tequila instead of dry gin.

TEQUILA FIZZ
2 oz. Gavilan Tequila
3/4 oz. Grenadine
1 tbsp. Lemon Juice
1 Egg White
Shake well with ice and strain into collins glass over ice cubes. Fill with ginger ale and stir.

TEQUILA MANHATTAN
2 oz. Gavilan Tequila
1 oz. Sweet Vermouth
1 dash Lime Juice
Shake with ice and strain over ice cubes in old-fashioned glass. Add a cherry and an orange slice.

TEQUILA MATADOR
1 1/2 oz. Gavilan Tequila
3 oz. Pineapple Juice
Juice of 1/2 Lime
Shake with crushed ice and strain into champagne glass.

TEQUILA MOCKINGBIRD
1 1/2 oz. Gavilan Tequila
3/4 oz. Mr. Boston
      Crème de Menthe
      (Green)
Juice of 1 Lime
Shake with ice and strain into cocktail glass. Decorate with a lime slice.

TEQUILA OLD FASHIONED
1 1/2 oz. Gavilan Tequila
1/2 tsp. Sugar
1 dash Bitters
Splash Carbonated Water
Mix sugar, bitters, and a teaspoon of water in old-fashioned glass. Add tequila, ice, and a splash of carbonated water. Decorate with a pineapple stick.

TEQUILA PINK
1 1/2 oz. Gavilan Tequila
1 oz. Dry Vermouth
1 dash Grenadine
Shake with ice and strain into cocktail glass.

TEQUILA PUNCH
1 Liter Gavilan Tequila
1 750ml bottle Shadow
      Creek Champagne
4 750ml bottles Sauterne
64 oz. Fresh Fruits
      (Cubes or Balls)
Sweeten to taste, chill thoroughly, and add ice cubes just before serving. Place in a large bowl and serve in sherbet cups.

TEQUILA SOUR

Juice of ½ Lemon
1 tsp. Powdered Sugar
2 oz. Gavilan Tequila

Shake with ice and strain into sour glass. Decorate with a half-slice of lemon and a cherry.

TEQUILA STRAIGHT

¼ Lemon
1 pinch Salt
1½ oz. Gavilan Tequila

Put salt between thumb and index finger on back of left hand. Hold jigger of tequila in same hand and the lemon wedge in right hand. Taste salt, drink the tequila, and then suck the lemon.

TEQUILA SUNRISE

2 oz. Gavilan Tequila
4 oz. Orange Juice
¾ oz. Grenadine

Stir tequila and orange juice with ice and strain into highball glass. Add ice cubes. Pour in grenadine slowly and allow to settle. Before drinking, stir to complete your sunrise.

TEQUINI

1½ oz. Gavilan Tequila
½ oz. Dry Vermouth
1 dash Bitters (if desired)

Stir with ice and strain into cocktail glass. Serve with a twist of lemon peel and an olive.

TEQUONIC

2 oz. Gavilan Tequila
Juice of ½ Lemon or Lime
Tonic

Pour tequila over ice cubes in old-fashioned glass. Add fruit juice, fill with tonic, and stir.

THANKSGIVING SPECIAL

¾ oz. Mr. Boston Apricot Flavored Brandy
¾ oz. Mr. Boston Gin
¾ oz. Dry Vermouth
¼ tsp. Lemon Juice

Shake with ice and strain into cocktail glass. Serve with a cherry.

THE SHOOT

1 oz. Desmond & Duff Scotch
1 oz. Dry Sherry
1 tsp. Orange Juice
1 tsp. Lemon Juice
½ tsp. Powdered Sugar

Shake with ice and strain into cocktail glass.

THIRD DEGREE COCKTAIL

1½ oz. Mr. Boston Gin
¾ oz. Dry Vermouth
1 tsp. Absinthe Substitute

Stir with ice and strain into cocktail glass.

THIRD RAIL COCKTAIL
$3/4$ oz. Mr. Boston Rum
$3/4$ oz. Mr. Boston Apple Brandy
$3/4$ oz. Mr. Boston Five Star Brandy
$1/4$ tsp. Absinthe Substitute
Shake with ice and strain into cocktail glass.

THISTLE COCKTAIL
$1^1/2$ oz. Sweet Vermouth
$1^1/2$ oz. Desmond & Duff Scotch
2 dashes Bitters
Stir with ice and strain into cocktail glass.

THREE MILLER COCKTAIL
$1^1/2$ oz. Mr. Boston Rum
$3/4$ oz. Mr. Boston Five Star Brandy
1 tsp. Grenadine
$1/4$ tsp. Lemon Juice
Shake with ice and strain into cocktail glass.

THREE STRIPES COCKTAIL
1 oz. Mr. Boston Gin
$1/2$ oz. Dry Vermouth
1 tbsp. Orange Juice
Shake with ice and strain into cocktail glass.

THUNDER
1 tsp. Powdered Sugar
1 Egg Yolk
$1^1/2$ oz. Mr. Boston Five Star Brandy
1 pinch Cayenne Pepper
Shake with ice and strain into cocktail glass.

THUNDER-AND-LIGHTNING
1 Egg Yolk
1 tsp. Powdered Sugar
$1^1/2$ oz. Mr. Boston Five Star Brandy
Shake with ice and strain into cocktail glass.

THUNDERCLAP
$3/4$ oz. Mr. Boston Gin
$3/4$ oz. Old Thompson Blended Whiskey
$3/4$ oz. Mr. Boston Five Star Brandy
Shake with ice and strain into cocktail glass.

TIDBIT
1 oz. Mr. Boston Gin
1 scoop Vanilla Ice Cream
1 dash Dry Sherry
Blend at low speed and pour into highball glass.

TIPPERARY COCKTAIL
$3/4$ oz. Irish Whisky
$3/4$ oz. Chartreuse (Green)
$3/4$ oz. Sweet Vermouth
Stir well with ice and strain into cocktail glass.

T.N.T. NO. 1
$1^1/2$ oz. Old Thompson Blended Whiskey
$1^1/2$ oz. Absinthe Substitute
Shake with ice and strain into cocktail glass.

T.N.T. NO. 2
1 oz. Gavilan Tequila
Tonic
Mix with ice in an old-fashioned glass.

TOASTED ALMOND
1½ oz. Expresso® Coffee
Liqueur
1 oz. Amaretto di
Saronno
1½ oz. Cream or Milk
Add all ingredients over ice
in an old-fashioned glass.

TODDIES
See Index on page 267 for
complete list of Toddy
recipes.

TOM-AND-JERRY
One Egg Separated
Powdered Sugar
Baking Soda
¼ oz. Mr. Boston Rum
First prepare batter, using
yolk and white of one egg,
beating each separately and
thoroughly. Then combine
both, adding enough
superfine powdered sugar
to stiffen. Add to this one
pinch of baking soda and
rum to preserve the batter.
Then add a little more
sugar to stiffen.
Hot Milk
1½ oz. Mr. Boston Rum
½ oz. Mr. Boston Five
Star Brandy
To serve, use hot Tom-and-
Jerry mug, using one
tablespoon of above batter,
dissolved in 3 tablespoons
hot milk. Add rum. Then
fill mug with hot milk
within ¼ inch of the top of
the mug and stir. Then top
with brandy and sprinkle a
little nutmeg on top. The
secret of a Tom-and-Jerry is
to have a stiff batter and a
warm mug.

TOMBOY
½ cup Chilled Tomato
Juice
½ cup Cold Beer
Pour tomato juice into
highball glass. Add beer.

TOM COLLINS
Juice of $^1/_2$ Lemon
1 tsp.   Powdered Sugar
2 oz.   Mr. Boston Gin
Shake with ice and strain
into collins glass. Add
several ice cubes, fill with
carbonated water, and stir.
Decorate with slices of
lemon, orange, and a
cherry. Serve with straw.

TOP BANANA
1 oz.   Mr. Boston Vodka
1 oz.   Mr. Boston
    Crème de Banana
Juice of $^1/_2$ Orange
Shake with ice and strain
into old-fashioned glass
over ice cubes.

TOREADOR
$1^1/_2$ oz. Gavilan Tequila
$^1/_2$ oz.   Mr. Boston
    Crème de Cacao
1 tbsp. Light Cream
Shake with ice and strain
into cocktail glass. Top with
a little whipped cream and
sprinkle lightly with cocoa.

TORRIDORA COCKTAIL
$1^1/_2$ oz. Mr. Boston Rum
$^1/_2$ oz.   Mr. Boston
    Coffee Flavored Brandy
$1^1/_2$ tsp. Light Cream
Shake with ice, strain into
cocktail glass. Float 1
teaspoon of 151 proof rum
on top.

TOVARICH COCKTAIL
$1^1/_2$ oz. Mr. Boston Vodka
$^3/_4$ oz.   Kümmel
Juice of $^1/_2$ Lime
Shake with ice and strain
into cocktail glass.

TRILBY COCKTAIL
$1^1/_2$ oz. Kentucky Tavern
    Bourbon
$^3/_4$ oz.   Sweet Vermouth
2 dashes Orange Bitters
Stir with ice and strain into
cocktail glass.

TRINITY COCKTAIL
$^3/_4$ oz.   Sweet Vermouth
$^3/_4$ oz.   Dry Vermouth
$^3/_4$ oz.   Mr. Boston Gin
Stir with ice and strain into
cocktail glass.

TROIS RIVIÈRES
$1^1/_2$ oz. Mr. Boston Five
    Star Canadian Whiskey
1 tbsp. Dubonnet®
$1^1/_2$ tsp. Mr. Boston Triple
    Sec
Shake with ice and strain
into old-fashioned glass
over ice cubes. Add a twist
of orange peel.

TROPICAL COCKTAIL
$^3/_4$ oz.   Mr. Boston
    Crème de Cacao
    (White)
$^3/_4$ oz.   Maraschino
$^3/_4$ oz.   Dry Vermouth
1 dash Bitters
Stir with ice and strain into
cocktail glass.

TULIP COCKTAIL

1½ tsp. Lemon Juice
1½ tsp. Mr. Boston Apricot Flavored Brandy
¾ oz.   Sweet Vermouth
¾ oz.   Mr. Boston Apple Brandy

Shake with ice and strain into cocktail glass.

TURF COCKTAIL

¼ tsp.   Absinthe Substitute
2 dashes Bitters
1 oz.   Dry Vermouth
1 oz.   Mr. Boston Gin

Stir with ice and strain into cocktail glass. Add a twist of orange peel.

TUXEDO COCKTAIL

1½ oz. Mr. Boston Gin
1½ oz. Dry Vermouth
¼ tsp.   Maraschino
¼ tsp.   Absinthe Substitute
2 dashes Orange Bitters

Stir with ice and strain into cocktail glass. Serve with a cherry.

TWIN HILLS

1½ oz. Old Thompson Blended Whiskey
2 tsp.   Benedictine
1½ tsp. Lemon Juice
1½ tsp. Lime Juice
1 tsp.   Sugar

Shake with ice and strain into sour glass. Add a slice of lime and of lemon.

TWIN SIX COCKTAIL

1 oz.   Mr. Boston Gin
½ oz.   Sweet Vermouth
¼ tsp.   Grenadine
1 tbsp. Orange Juice
1 Egg White

Shake with ice and strain into cocktail glass.

TWISTER

2 oz.   Mr. Boston Vodka
Juice of ⅓ Lime
Lemon Soda

Pour vodka and lime into collins glass. Add several ice cubes and drop a lime rind into glass. Fill with lemon soda and stir.

TYPHOON

1 oz.   Mr. Boston Gin
½ oz.   Mr. Boston Anisette
1 oz.   Lime Juice
Shadow Creek Champagne

Shake all ingredients, except champagne, with ice. Strain into collins glass with ice cubes. Fill glass with chilled champagne.

U

ULANDA COCKTAIL

1½ oz. Mr. Boston Gin
¾ oz. Mr. Boston Triple Sec
¼ tsp. Absinthe Substitute

Stir with ice and strain into cocktail glass.

UNION JACK COCKTAIL

¾ oz. Mr. Boston Sloe Gin
1½ oz. Mr. Boston Gin
½ tsp. Grenadine

Shake with ice and strain into cocktail glass.

V

VALENCIA COCKTAIL
1 tbsp. Orange Juice
1¹/₂ oz. Mr. Boston
     Apricot Flavored
     Brandy
2 dashes Orange Bitters
Shake with ice and strain
into cocktail glass.

VANDERBILT COCKTAIL
³/₄ oz. Mr. Boston
     Cherry Flavored
     Brandy
1¹/₂ oz. Mr. Boston Five
     Star Brandy
1 tsp. Sugar Syrup
2 dashes Bitters
Stir with ice and strain into
cocktail glass.

VAN VLEET
3 oz. Mr. Boston Rum
1 oz. Maple Syrup
1 oz. Lemon Juice
Shake well with ice and
strain into old-fashioned
glass over ice cubes.

VELVET HAMMER NO. 1
1¹/₂ oz. Mr. Boston Vodka
1 tbsp. Mr. Boston
     Crème de Cacao
1 tbsp. Light Cream
Shake with ice and strain
into cocktail glass.

VELVET HAMMER NO. 2

1½ oz. Strega
1 oz.   Mr. Boston
        Crème de Cacao
        (White)
1 tbsp. Light Cream

Shake with ice and strain into cocktail glass.

VERBOTEN

1½ oz. Mr. Boston Gin
1 tbsp. Forbidden Fruit
1 tbsp. Orange Juice
1 tbsp. Lemon Juice

Shake with ice and strain into cocktail glass. Add brandied cherry.

VERMOUTH CASSIS

3/4 oz. Mr. Boston
        Crème de Cassis
1½ oz. Dry Vermouth

Stir in highball glass with ice cubes and fill with carbonated water. Stir again and serve.

VERMOUTH COCKTAIL

1 oz.   Dry Vermouth
1 oz.   Sweet Vermouth
1 dash Orange Bitters

Stir with ice and strain into cocktail glass. Serve with a cherry.

VESUVIO

1 oz.   Mr. Boston Rum
Juice of ½ Lemon
1 tsp. Powdered Sugar
½ Egg White
½ oz.   Sweet Vermouth

Shake with ice and strain into old-fashioned glass over ice cubes.

VICTOR

1½ oz. Mr. Boston Gin
½ oz.   Mr. Boston Five
        Star Brandy
½ oz.   Sweet Vermouth

Shake with ice and strain into cocktail glass.

VICTORY COLLINS

1½ oz. Mr. Boston Vodka
3 oz.   Unsweetened
        Grape Juice
3 oz.   Lemon Juice
1 tsp. Powdered Sugar

Shake with ice and strain into collins glass with ice cubes. Add a slice of orange.

VIRGIN

1 oz.   Mr. Boston Gin
½ oz.   Mr. Boston
        Crème de Menthe
        (White)
1 oz.   Forbidden Fruit

Shake with ice and strain into cocktail glass.

VIVA VILLA
Juice of 1 Lime
1 tsp. Sugar
1½ oz. Gavilan Tequila
Shake with ice and strain over ice cubes into old-fashioned glass, rimmed with salt.

VODKA AND APPLE JUICE
Put two or three cubes of ice into highball glass. Add 2 oz. Mr. Boston Vodka. Fill balance of glass with apple juice and stir.

VODKA AND TONIC
Pour 2 oz. Mr. Boston Vodka into highball glass over ice cubes. Add tonic and stir.

VODKA COLLINS
Make same as Tom Collins (see page 174) but use Mr. Boston Vodka instead of gin.

VODKA COOLER
Make same as Gin Cooler (see page 88) but use Mr. Boston Vodka instead of gin.

VODKA DAISY
Juice of ½ Lemon
½ tsp. Powdered Sugar
1 tsp. Grenadine
2 oz. Mr. Boston Vodka
Shake with ice and strain into stein or metal cup. Add ice cubes and decorate with fruit.

VODKA GIMLET
Make same as Gimlet (see page 88) but use Mr. Boston Vodka instead of gin.

VODKA GRASSHOPPER
3/4 oz. Mr. Boston Vodka
3/4 oz. Mr. Boston Crème de Menthe (Green)
3/4 oz. Mr. Boston Crème de Cacao (White)
Shake with ice and strain into cocktail glass.

VODKA MARTINI
See Special Martini Section on pages 204 and 206.

VODKA ON THE ROCKS
Put two or three cubes of ice in old-fashioned glass and add 2 oz. Mr. Boston Vodka. Serve with a twist of lemon peel.

VODKA SALTY DOG
1½ oz. Mr. Boston Vodka
5 oz. Grapefruit Juice
¼ tsp. Salt
Pour into highball glass over ice cubes. Stir well.

VODKA "7"
2 oz.   Mr. Boston Vodka
Juice of 1/2 Lime
   Carbonated Water

Pour lime and vodka into collins glass over ice cubes. Drop a lime rind in glass, fill balance with lemon soda, and stir.

VODKA SLING
Make same as Gin Sling (see page 89) but use **Mr. Boston Vodka** instead of gin.

VODKA SOUR
Juice of 1/2 Lemon
1/2 tsp. Powdered Sugar
2 oz.   Mr. Boston Vodka

Shake with ice and strain into sour glass. Decorate with a half-slice of lemon and a cherry.

VODKA STINGER
1 oz.   Mr. Boston Vodka
1 oz.   Mr. Boston
   Crème de Menthe
   (White)

Shake with ice and strain into cocktail glass.

W

WAIKIKI BEACHCOMBER
¾ oz. Mr. Boston Gin
¾ oz. Mr. Boston Triple Sec
1 tbsp. Fresh Pineapple Juice

Shake with ice and strain into cocktail glass.

WALLICK COCKTAIL
1½ oz. Dry Vermouth
1½ oz. Mr. Boston Gin
1 tsp. Mr. Boston Triple Sec

Stir with ice and strain into cocktail glass.

WALLIS BLUE COCKTAIL
1 oz. Mr. Boston Triple Sec
1 oz. Mr. Boston Gin
Juice of 1 Lime

Moisten rim of an old-fashioned glass with lime juice and dip into powdered sugar. Shake ingredients with ice and strain into prepared glass over ice cubes.

WALTERS
1½ oz. Desmond & Duff Scotch
1 tbsp. Orange Juice
1 tbsp. Lemon Juice

Shake with ice and strain into cocktail glass.

WARD EIGHT
Juice of ½ Lemon
1 tsp. Powdered Sugar
1 tsp. Grenadine
2 oz. Old Thompson Blended Whiskey

Shake with ice and strain into goblet filled with cracked ice. Add slices of orange, lemon, and a cherry. Serve with straws.

WARSAW COCKTAIL
1½ oz. Mr. Boston Vodka
½ oz. Mr. Boston Blackberry Flavored Brandy
½ oz. Dry Vermouth
1 tsp. Lemon Juice

Shake with ice and strain into cocktail glass.

WASHINGTON COCKTAIL

1½ oz. Dry Vermouth
¾ oz. Mr. Boston Five Star Brandy
2 dashes Bitters
½ tsp. Sugar Syrup

Stir with ice and strain into cocktail glass.

WASSAIL BOWL

2 cups Water
1 tsp. Freshly Ground Nutmeg
2 tsp. Ground Ginger
2 sticks of Cinnamon
6 whole Cloves
6 Allspice Berries
4 Coriander Seeds
4 Cardamom Seeds
2 750ml bottles Balfour Cream Sherry
64 oz. Ale
4 cups Sugar
12 Eggs Separated
1 cup Mr. Boston Five Star Brandy
12 Roasted Apple Slices or 12 Tiny Roasted Apples

Combine water and spices in a large saucepan and simmer for 10 minutes. Add sherry and ale and stir in sugar. Heat, but do not boil. Beat 12 egg yolks until they are pale and thick; fold in 12 stiffly beaten egg whites. Strain half the ale and sherry mixture over the eggs. Pour into a warmed punch bowl. Bring the remaining hot mixture to a boil and strain into punch bowl. Add brandy and apples.

WATERBURY COCKTAIL

$^1/_2$ tsp. Powdered Sugar
Juice of $^1/_4$ Lemon or
$^1/_2$ Lime
1 Egg White
1$^1/_2$ oz. Mr. Boston Five
Star Brandy
$^1/_2$ tsp. Grenadine

Shake with ice and strain into cocktail glass.

WATERLOO

1 oz. Mr. Boston Light
Rum
3 oz. Orange Juice
$^1/_2$ oz. Mandarine
Napoleon Liqueur

Pour rum and orange juice over ice in an old-fashioned glass. Stir. Float Mandarine Napoleon on top.

WATERMELON

Equal Parts:
Mr. Boston Vodka
Strawberry Liqueur
Sweet and Sour Mix
Orange Juice

Serve over ice in a collins glass.

WEBSTER COCKTAIL

Juice of $^1/_2$ Lime
1$^1/_2$ tsp. Mr. Boston
Apricot Flavored
Brandy
$^1/_2$ oz. Dry Vermouth
1 oz. Mr. Boston Gin

Shake with ice and strain into cocktail glass.

WEDDING BELLE COCKTAIL

1$^1/_2$ tsp. Orange Juice
1$^1/_2$ tsp. Mr. Boston
Cherry Flavored
Brandy
$^3/_4$ oz. Mr. Boston Gin
$^3/_4$ oz. Dubonnet®

Shake with ice and strain into cocktail glass.

WEEP-NO-MORE COCKTAIL

Juice of $^1/_2$ Lime
$^3/_4$ oz. Dubonnet®
$^3/_4$ oz. Mr. Boston Five
Star Brandy
$^1/_4$ tsp. Maraschino

Shake with ice and strain into cocktail glass.

WEMBLY COCKTAIL

$^3/_4$ oz. Dry Vermouth
1$^1/_2$ oz. Mr. Boston Gin
$^1/_4$ tsp. Mr. Boston
Apricot Flavored
Brandy
$^1/_2$ tsp. Mr. Boston Apple
Brandy

Stir with ice and strain into cocktail glass.

WESTERN ROSE

$^1/_2$ oz. Mr. Boston
Apricot Flavored
Brandy
1 oz. Mr. Boston Gin
$^1/_2$ oz. Dry Vermouth
$^1/_4$ tsp. Lemon Juice

Shake with ice and strain into cocktail glass.

WEST INDIAN PUNCH

- 64 oz. Mr. Boston Rum
- 1 750ml Mr. Boston Crème de Banana
- 32 oz. Pineapple Juice
- 32 oz. Orange Juice
- 32 oz. Lemon Juice
- 3/4 cup Powdered Sugar
- 1 tsp. Grated Nutmeg
- 1 tsp. Cinnamon
- 1/2 tsp. Grated Cloves
- 6 oz. Carbonated Water

Dissolve sugar and spices in carbonated water. Pour into large punchbowl over a block of ice, and add other ingredients. Stir and decorate with sliced bananas.

WHAT THE HELL

- 1 oz. Mr. Boston Gin
- 1 oz. Dry Vermouth
- 1 oz. Mr. Boston Apricot Flavored Brandy
- 1 dash Lemon Juice

Stir in old-fashioned glass over ice cubes.

WHIP COCKTAIL

- 1/2 oz. Dry Vermouth
- 1/2 oz. Sweet Vermouth
- 1 1/2 oz. Mr. Boston Five Star Brandy
- 1/4 tsp. Absinthe Substitute
- 1 tsp. Mr. Boston Triple Sec

Stir with ice and strain into cocktail glass.

WHISKEY COBBLER

Dissolve one teaspoon powdered sugar in 2 oz. carbonated water in a goblet. Fill with shaved ice and add 2 oz. Old Thompson Blended Whiskey. Stir and decorate with fruits in season. Serve with straw.

WHISKEY COCKTAIL

- 1 dash Bitters
- 1 tsp. Sugar Syrup
- 2 oz. Old Thompson Blended Whiskey

Stir with ice and strain into cocktail glass. Serve with a cherry.

WHISKEY COLLINS

- Juice of 1/2 Lemon
- 1 tsp. Powdered Sugar
- 2 oz. Old Thompson Blended Whiskey

Shake with ice and strain into collins glass. Add several ice cubes, fill with carbonated water, and stir. Decorate with slices of lemon, orange, and a cherry. Serve with straw.

WHISKEY DAISY

- Juice of 1/2 Lemon
- 1/2 tsp. Powdered Sugar
- 1 tsp. Grenadine
- 2 oz. Old Thompson Blended Whiskey

Shake with ice and strain into stein or metal cup. Add one ice cube and decorate with fruit.

Whiskey Squirt

WHISKEY EGGNOG

1 Whole Egg
1 tsp. Powdered Sugar
2 oz. Old Thompson
  Blended Whiskey

Shake ingredients with ice and strain into collins glass. Fill glass with milk. Sprinkle nutmeg on top.

WHISKEY FIX

Juice of 1/2 Lemon
1 tsp. Powdered Sugar

Shake with ice and strain into highball glass. Fill glass with ice. Add 2 1/2 oz. Old Thompson Blended Whiskey. Stir and add a slice of lemon. Serve with straws.

WHISKEY FLIP

1 Whole Egg
1 tsp. Powdered Sugar
1 1/2 oz. Old Thompson
  Blended Whiskey
2 tsp. Light Cream (if
  desired)

Shake with ice and strain into flip glass. Sprinkle a little nutmeg on top.

WHISKEY HIGHBALL

Pour 2 oz. Old Thompson Blended Whiskey into highball glass over ice cubes and fill with ginger ale or carbonated water. Add a twist of lemon peel, if desired, and stir.

WHISKEY MILK PUNCH

1 tsp. Powdered Sugar
2 oz. Old Thompson
  Blended Whiskey
8 oz. Milk

Shake with ice, strain into collins glass, and sprinkle nutmeg on top.

WHISKEY ORANGE

Juice of 1/2 Orange
1 tsp. Powdered Sugar
1/2 tsp. Absinthe
  Substitute
1 1/2 oz. Old Thompson
  Blended Whiskey

Shake with ice and strain into highball glass over ice cubes. Decorate with slices of orange and lemon.

WHISKEY RICKEY

Juice of 1/2 Lime
1 1/2 oz. Old Thompson
  Blended Whiskey

Pour into highball glass over ice cubes and fill with carbonated water. Stir. Drop the lime rind into glass.

WHISKEY SANGAREE

In an old-fashioned glass, dissolve 1/2 teaspoon powdered sugar in 1 teaspoon of water and add 2 oz. Old Thompson Blended Whiskey. Add ice cubes and a splash of carbonated water. Stir and float a tablespoon of port on top. Sprinkle lightly with nutmeg.

WHISKEY SKIN ▯
Put lump of sugar into hot whiskey glass and fill two-thirds with boiling water. Add **2 oz. Old Thompson Blended Whiskey**. Stir, then add a twist of lemon peel.

WHISKEY SLING ▯
In an old-fashioned glass, dissolve one teaspoon powdered sugar in one teaspoon of water and juice of $\frac{1}{2}$ lemon; add ice cubes and **2 oz. Old Thompson Blended Whiskey**. Stir and add a twist of lemon peel.

WHISKEY SMASH ▯
Muddle one lump of sugar in an old-fashioned glass with 1 oz. carbonated water and 4 sprigs of mint. Add **2 oz. Old Thompson Blended Whiskey**, then ice cubes. Stir and decorate with a slice of orange and a cherry. Add a twist of lemon peel.

WHISKEY SOUR
▯ Juice of $\frac{1}{2}$ Lemon
$\frac{1}{2}$ tsp. Powdered Sugar
2 oz. Old Thompson Blended Whiskey
Shake with ice and strain into sour glass. Decorate with a half-slice of lemon and a cherry.

WHISKEY SQUIRT
▯ $1\frac{1}{2}$ oz. Old Thompson Blended Whiskey
1 tbsp. Powdered Sugar
1 tbsp. Grenadine
Shake with ice and strain into highball glass and fill with carbonated water and ice cubes. Decorate with cubes of pineapple and strawberries.

WHISKEY SWIZZLE
Make same as Gin Swizzle (see page 90) using **2 oz. Old Thompson Blended Whiskey** instead of gin.

WHISKEY TODDY (COLD)
▯ $\frac{1}{2}$ tsp. Powdered Sugar
2 tsp. Water
2 oz. Old Thompson Blended Whiskey
Stir sugar and water in an old-fashioned glass. Add ice cubes and whiskey, and stir. Add a twist of lemon peel.

WHISKEY TODDY (HOT)
Put lump of sugar into hot whiskey glass and fill two-thirds with boiling water. Add **2 oz. Old Thompson Blended Whiskey**. Stir and decorate with a slice of lemon. Sprinkle nutmeg on top. ▯

WHISPERS-OF-THE-FROST COCKTAIL

¾ oz. Old Thompson Blended Whiskey

¾ oz. Balfour Cream Sherry

¾ oz. Port

1 tsp. Powdered Sugar

Stir with ice and strain into cocktail glass. Serve with slices of lemon and orange.

WHITE CARGO COCKTAIL

1 scoop Vanilla Ice Cream

1 oz. Mr. Boston Gin

Shake until thoroughly mixed and add water or sauterne if the mixture is too thick. Serve in an old-fashioned glass.

WHITE ELEPHANT

1½ oz. Mr. Boston Gin

1 oz. Sweet Vermouth

1 Egg White

Shake with ice and strain into cocktail glass.

WHITE LADY

1 Egg White

1 tsp. Powdered Sugar

1 tsp. Light Cream

1½ oz. Mr. Boston Gin

Shake with ice and strain into cocktail glass.

WHITE LILY COCKTAIL

¾ oz. Mr. Boston Triple Sec

¾ oz. Mr. Boston Rum

¾ oz. Mr. Boston Gin

¼ tsp. Mr. Boston Anisette

Shake with ice and strain into cocktail glass.

WHITE LION COCKTAIL

Juice of ½ Lemon

1 tsp. Powdered Sugar

2 dashes Bitters

½ tsp. Grenadine

1½ oz. Mr. Boston Rum

Shake with ice and strain into cocktail glass.

WHITE PLUSH

2 oz. Old Thompson Blended Whiskey

1 cup Milk

1 tsp. Powdered Sugar

Shake with ice and strain into collins glass.

WHITE ROSE COCKTAIL

¾ oz. Mr. Boston Gin

1 tbsp. Orange Juice

Juice of 1 Lime

½ oz. Maraschino

1 Egg White

Shake with ice and strain into cocktail glass.

White Russian

WHITE RUSSIAN
1 oz.   Expresso® Coffee
      Liqueur
2 oz.   Mr. Boston Vodka
Milk or Cream

Put coffee liqueur and vodka in an old-fashioned glass over ice cubes and fill with milk or cream.

WHITE WAY COCKTAIL
3/4 oz.   Mr. Boston
        Creme de Menthe
        (White)
1 1/2 oz.   Mr. Boston Gin

Shake with ice and strain into cocktail glass.

WHY NOT?
1 oz.   Mr. Boston Gin
1 oz.   Mr. Boston
      Apricot Flavored
      Brandy
1/2 oz.   Dry Vermouth
1 dash   Lemon Juice

Shake with ice and strain into cocktail glass.

WIDOW'S DREAM
1 1/2 oz.   Benedictine
1 Whole Egg

Shake with ice and strain into cocktail glass. Float one teaspoon of sweet cream on top.

WIDOW'S KISS
1 oz.   Mr. Boston Five
      Star Brandy
1/2 oz.   Chartreuse
        (Yellow)
1/2 oz.   Benedictine
1 dash   Bitters

Shake with ice and strain into cocktail glass.

WILL ROGERS
1 1/2 oz.   Mr. Boston Gin
1 tbsp.   Orange Juice
1/2 oz.   Dry Vermouth
1 dash   Mr. Boston Triple
        Sec

Shake with ice and strain into cocktail glass.

WINDY CORNER COCKTAIL
Stir 2 oz. Mr. Boston Blackberry Flavored Brandy with ice and strain into cocktail glass. Sprinkle a little nutmeg on top.

WINE COOLER
Pour 3 oz. red Corbett Canyon Vineyard wine into wine glass with ice cubes. Fill balance with lemon-lime soda, or preferred clear carbonated soda and stir.

WOODSTOCK
1 1/2 oz.   Mr. Boston Gin
1 oz.   Lemon Juice
1 1/2 tsp.   Maple Syrup
1 dash   Orange Bitters

Shake with ice and strain into cocktail glass.

WOODWARD COCKTAIL
1 1/2 oz.   Desmond & Duff
        Scotch
1/2 oz.   Dry Vermouth
1 tbsp.   Grapefruit Juice

Shake with ice and strain into cocktail glass.

X

XANTHIA COCKTAIL
¾ oz. Mr. Boston
Cherry Flavored
Brandy
¾ oz. Chartreuse
(Yellow)
¾ oz. Mr. Boston Gin
Stir with ice and strain into
cocktail glass.

XERES COCKTAIL
1 dash Orange Bitters
2 oz. Dry Sherry
Stir with ice and strain into
cocktail glass.

X.Y.Z. COCKTAIL
1 tbsp. Lemon Juice
½ oz. Mr. Boston Triple
Sec
1 oz. Mr. Boston Rum
Shake with ice and strain
into cocktail glass.

Y

YALE COCKTAIL
$1\frac{1}{2}$ oz. Mr. Boston Gin
$\frac{1}{2}$ oz. Dry Vermouth
1 dash Bitters
1 tsp. Blue Curacao
Stir with ice and strain into cocktail glass.

YELLOW PARROT COCKTAIL
$\frac{3}{4}$ oz. Mr. Boston Anisette
$\frac{3}{4}$ oz. Chartreuse (Yellow)
$\frac{3}{4}$ oz. Mr. Boston Apricot Flavored Brandy
Shake with ice and strain into cocktail glass.

YELLOW RATTLER
1 oz. Mr. Boston Gin
1 tbsp. Orange Juice
$\frac{1}{2}$ oz. Dry Vermouth
$\frac{1}{2}$ oz. Sweet Vermouth
Shake with ice and strain into cocktail glass. Add a cocktail onion.

YOLANDA
$\frac{1}{2}$ oz. Mr. Boston Five Star Brandy
$\frac{1}{2}$ oz. Mr. Boston Gin
$\frac{1}{2}$ oz. Mr. Boston Anisette
1 oz. Sweet Vermouth
1 dash Grenadine
Shake with ice and strain into cocktail glass. Add a twist of orange peel.

Z

ZAZA COCKTAIL
$1^1/_2$ oz. Mr. Boston Gin
$^3/_4$ oz. Dubonnet®
Stir with ice and strain into cocktail glass. Add a twist of orange peel.

ZERO MIST
For each serving chill **2 oz. Mr. Boston Crème de Menthe (Green)** mixed with 1 oz. water in freezer compartment of refrigerator for 2 hours or longer, if desired. (Does not have to be frozen solid.) Serve in cocktail glasses.

ZOMBIE
1 oz.   Unsweetened Pineapple Juice
Juice of 1 Lime
Juice of 1 Small Orange
1 tsp.   Powdered Sugar
$^1/_2$ oz.   Mr. Boston Apricot Flavored Brandy
$2^1/_2$ oz. Mr. Boston Rum
1 oz.   Jamaica Rum
1 oz.   Passion Fruit Syrup (if desired)
Put all ingredients with a half cup of crushed ice into an electric blender. Blend at low speed for one minute and strain into frosted highball glass. Decorate with a stick of pineapple and one green and one red cherry. Carefully float $^1/_2$ oz. 151 proof rum and then top with sprig of fresh mint dipped in powdered sugar. Serve with straw.

NEW DRINKS

ALABAMA SLAMMER
1 oz.   Amaretto di Saronno
1 oz.   Southern Comfort
1/2 oz.   Mr. Boston Sloe Gin

Stir in a highball glass over ice and add a splash of lemon juice.

FERRARI
1 oz.   Amaretto di Saronno
2 oz.   Dry Vermouth

Mix in an old-fashioned glass on the rocks and add a lemon twist.

GOLDEN FRIENDSHIP
Equal Parts:
Amaretto di Saronno
Sweet Vermouth
Mr. Boston Light Rum

Mix in a collins glass over ice and fill with ginger ale. Garnish with an orange spiral and a cherry.

HUMMER
1 oz.   Expresso® Coffee Liqueur
1 oz.   Mr. Boston Light Rum
2 large scoops Vanilla Ice Cream

Blend briefly and serve in highball glass.

INDIAN SUMMER
Wet flip glass edge and rim and then dip in cinnamon. Add 2 ounces Mr. Boston Apple Schnapps. Top off with hot apple cider. Add cinnamon stick if desired.

KAMIKAZE
1 oz.   Lime Juice
1 oz.   Mr. Boston Triple Sec
1 oz.   Mr. Boston Vodka

Shake and serve over ice in old-fashioned glass.

MELON BALL
1 oz.   Melon Liqueur
1 oz.   Mr. Boston Vodka
2 oz.   Pineapple Juice

Pour over ice in a highball glass and garnish with an orange, pineapple, or watermelon slice.

Strawberry Fields Forever, Alabama Slammer, Kamikaze, Toasted Almond, and Melon Ball

Golden Friendship, Hummer, Ferrari, Indian Summer, and Saronno Colada

SARONNO COLADA (NUTTY COLADA)

3 oz.   Amaretto di Saronno
3 tbsp. Coconut Milk
3 tbsp. Crushed Pineapple

Put in an electric blender with 2 cups of crushed ice and blend at high speed for a short time. Pour into a collins glass and serve with a straw.

STRAWBERRY FIELDS FOREVER

2 oz.   Mr. Boston Original Strawberry Schnapps
$1/2$ oz.   Mr. Boston Five Star Brandy

Pour over ice in a highball glass. Fill with carbonated water. Garnish with a fresh strawberry.

TOASTED ALMOND

$1^1/_2$ oz. Expresso® Coffee Liqueur
1 oz.   Amaretto di Saronno
$1^1/_2$ oz. Cream or Milk

Add all ingredients over ice in an old-fashioned glass.

SPECIAL SECTIONS

Eggnog

AMBASSADOR'S MORNING LIFT
- 32 oz. Prepared Dairy Eggnog
- 6 oz. Cognac
- 3 oz. Jamaica Rum
- 3 oz. Mr. Boston Crème de Cacao (Brown)

Mr. Boston Five Star Brandy or Kentucky Tavern Bourbon may be substituted for cognac.

BALTIMORE EGGNOG
- 32 oz. Prepared Dairy Eggnog
- 5 oz. Mr. Boston Five Star Brandy
- 5 oz. Jamaica Rum
- 5 oz. Madeira Wine

BRANDY EGGNOG
- 32 oz. Prepared Dairy Eggnog
- 12 oz. Mr. Boston Five Star Brandy

BREAKFAST EGGNOG
- 32 oz. Prepared Dairy Eggnog
- 10 oz. Mr. Boston Apricot Flavored Brandy
- 2½ oz. Mr. Boston Triple Sec

CHRISTMAS YULE EGGNOG
- 32 oz. Prepared Dairy Eggnog
- 12 oz. Old Thompson Blended Whiskey
- 1½ oz. Mr. Boston Rum

GENERAL HARRISON'S EGGNOG
- 32 oz. Prepared Dairy Eggnog
- 24 oz. Sweet Cider

IMPERIAL EGGNOG
- 32 oz. Prepared Dairy Eggnog
- 10 oz. Mr. Boston Five Star Brandy
- 2 oz. Mr. Boston Apricot Flavored Brandy

Eggnog

NASHVILLE EGGNOG
- 32 oz. Prepared Dairy Eggnog
- 6 oz. Kentucky Tavern Bourbon
- 3 oz. Mr. Boston Five Star Brandy
- 3 oz. Jamaica Rum

PORT WINE EGGNOG
- 32 oz. Prepared Dairy Eggnog
- 18 oz. Port Wine

RUM EGGNOG
- 32 oz. Prepared Dairy Eggnog
- 12 oz. Mr. Boston Rum

SHERRY EGGNOG
- 32 oz. Prepared Dairy Eggnog
- 18 oz. Balfour Cream Sherry

WHISKEY EGGNOG
- 32 oz. Prepared Dairy Eggnog
- 12 oz. Old Thompson Blended Whiskey

Summer Drinks—Planter's Punch, Sangria, California Lemonade, and Champagne Sherbet Punch

Winter Drinks—Irish Coffee, Mulled Claret, Cherry Rum and Hot
Tom-and-Jerry

Martinis

**MARTINI
(Traditional 2-to-1)**
1½ oz. Mr. Boston Gin
¾ oz.　Dry Vermouth
Serve with an olive

**DRY MARTINI
(5-to-1)**
1⅔ oz. Mr. Boston Gin
⅓ oz.　Dry Vermouth
Serve with an olive.

**EXTRA DRY MARTINI
(8-to-1)**
2 oz.　Mr. Boston Gin
¼ oz.　Dry Vermouth
Serve with an olive.

MARTINI (SWEET)
1 oz.　Mr. Boston Gin
1 oz.　Sweet Vermouth
Serve with an olive

VODKA MARTINI
Substitute Mr. Boston
Vodka for Mr. Boston Gin
in any of these Martini
recipes.

MARTINI (Medium)
1½ oz. Mr. Boston Gin
½ oz.　Dry Vermouth
½ oz.　Sweet Vermouth
Serve with an olive.

BOSTON BULLET
A Martini substituting an
olive stuffed with an
almond for the regular
olive.

DILLATINI
A Martini substituting a
dilly bean in place of the
olive.

Martini on-the-rocks with a twist

GIBSON
This is a Dry or Extra Dry Martini with a twist of lemon peel and served with one to three pearl onions. May also be made with Mr. Boston Vodka.

TEQUINI
A Martini made with tequila instead of dry gin. Serve with a twist of lemon peel and an olive.

RUM MARTINI
4 to 5 part Mr. Boston Rum
Dash Dry Vermouth
Serve on the rocks with a twist of lemon.

SAKE MARTINI—SAKINI
1 part Sake
3 parts Mr. Boston Gin
Stir with ice, strain into 3 or 4 oz. cocktail glass, and serve with an olive.

THE LIQUOR DICTIONARY

Much of the enjoyment of social drinking comes from a knowledge of the different types of alcoholic beverages available. This section was prepared to help you understand some of the subtle differences between one type of liquor and another.

First, here are a few common terms frequently misunderstand:

Alcohol (C_2H_5OH)—the common ingredient of all liquor. There are many types of alcohol, but for liquor only ethyl alcohol is used. Of the several types of ethyl alcohol, those spirits distilled from grain, grape, fruit, and cane are the most common.

Proof—a measurement of alcoholic strength or content. One degree of proof equals one-half of one percent of alcohol. An 80 proof product contains forty percent alcohol by volume; a 90 proof product, forty-five percent alcohol, etc.

For centuries the Scotch, British Gin, and Canadian Whisky sold in England, Scotland, and most of the rest of the world was 80 proof. America has only begun to appreciate the tasteful quality of the more moderate lower proofs. Practically all of the rum sold in America is now 80 proof and vodka at 80 proof outsells higher proof vodkas. For years the most expensive, famous name cognacs have been imported at 80 proof, and now nearly all American-made brandy is also 80 proof.

Grain Neutral Spirits is a practically tasteless, colorless, alcohol distilled from grain (like whiskey) but at 190 proof or above, whereas whiskey must be distilled at less than 190 proof. Used in blended whiskies, in making gin and vodkas, and in many other liquors.

Brandy

Brandy—is distilled from a fermented mash of grapes or other fruit, aged in oak casks, and usually bottled at 80 proof. Long enjoyed as an after-dinner drink, brandy is also widely used in mixed drinks and cooking.

Cognac—this fine brandy, known for its smoothness and heady dry aroma, is produced only in the cognac region of France. (All cognac is brandy, but not all brandy is cognac, nor is all French brandy cognac.)

Armagnac—is much like cognac but has a drier taste. It is produced only in the Armagnac region of France.

American Brandy—all of which is distilled in California, has its own taste characteristics. Unlike European brandies (whose farmer-distillers sell their brandies to the blender-shippers who control the brand names), California brandies are usually produced by individual firms that grow the grapes, distill, age, blend, bottle, and market the brandies under their own brand names.

Apple Brandy, Apple Jack, or Calvados—is distilled from a cider made from apples. Calvados is produced only in Normandy, France. Apple Jack may be bottled-in-bond under the same regulations that apply to whiskey.

Fruit Flavored Brandies—are brandy-based liqueurs produced from blackberries, peaches, apricots, cherries, and ginger. They are usually bottled at 70 or 80 proof.

Liqueurs

The words liqueur and cordial are synonymous, describing liquors made by mixing or redistilling neutral spirits, brandy, whiskey, or other spirits with fruits, flowers, herbs, seeds, roots, plants, or juices to which sweetening has been added. Practically all liqueurs are sweet and colorful, with highly concentrated, dessertlike flavor.

Liqueurs are made in all countries. Several, made from closely guarded secret recipes and processes, are known throughout the world by their trade or proprietary brand names.

Here are brief descriptions of the liqueurs and flavorings mentioned most frequently in the recipes in this book.

Absinthe—anise seed (licorice) flavor; contains wormwood (illegal in the United States)

Absinthe Substitutes—Abisante, Abson, Anisette, Herbsaint, Mistra, Ojen, Oxygene, Pernod

Amaretto di Saronno—the original Italian almond-flavored liqueur

Amer Picon—bitter, orange-flavored French cordial made from quinine and spices

Benedictine—secret herb formula first produced by Benedictine monks

Chartreuse—yellow and green herb liqueurs developed by Carthusian monks

Cream Liqueurs—a relatively recent addition to the category. Usually flavored with chocolate, coffee, or orange.

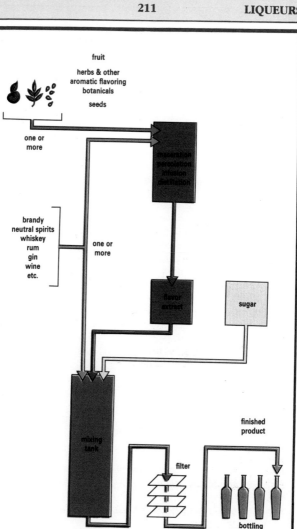

I. How Liqueur Is Made

Crème(s)—so called because high sugar content results in cream-like consistency
Crème de Cacao—from cacao and vanilla beans
Crème de Cassis—from black currants
Crème de Menthe—from mint
Crème de Noyaux—from almonds

Curaçao—orange-flavored, made from dried orange peel, from Dutch West Indies. May be blue or orange in color.

Forbidden Fruit—a domestic liqueur produced by blending shaddock fruit (a type of grapefruit) and imported cognac.

Kümmel—caraway and anise seeds and other herb flavors

Mandarine Napoleon—cognac-based mandarine orange flavor

Maraschino—liqueur made from cherries grown in Dalmatia, Yugoslavia

Rock and Rye—sweetened rye whiskey sometimes bottled with rock candy or fruit slices.

Schnapps—light bodied liqueur, now available in a wide variety of flavors

Sloe Gin—a liqueur made from sloe berries (blackthorn bush)

Strega—Italian liqueur

Swedish Punch—Scandinavian liqueur made from Batavia Arak rum, tea, lemon, and other spices. Also known as Arrack Punsch and Caloric Punch (the latter because it gives off heat).

Triple Sec—colorless Curaçao, but less sweet. Orange flavor.

Gin

Gin was originally sold in apothecary shops as a medicine to cleanse the blood of disease. Whether or not it accomplished that purpose became irrelevant—people *felt* better, so in the 17th century the English took the Dutch medicine back to their country and drank it liberally with or without toasting anyone's health.

Gins are little more than neutral spirits distilled from grain. But they are reprocessed and redistilled with a flavorist's grab-bag of assorted herbs and spices with the main ingredient being juniper berries. Each "secret formula" creates a distinctively flavored gin.

English gins are 94 proof; American gins are 80 to 94 proof. Either way the two drinks are equally dry, which means unsweetened. Most gins are not aged.

Rum

Rum is made from sugar cane boiled down to a rich residue called molasses which is then fermented and distilled.

Light rum is lighter in color and flavor. Dry, light rums are traditionally produced in Spanish-speaking islands like Puerto Rico.

Dark rum results from the addition of caramel coloring or aging. It has a heavier flavor and comes from the tropics: Jamaica, Haiti, or Martinique.

Rums are aged from three to ten years (though some of the very light rums leave the cask in two years).

Besides being the favorite drink of pirates and the punch in Planter's Punch, rum can be substituted in most cocktails calling for gin or vodka. (The lighter the rum the better.)

There are also 151 proof rums that are excellent in desserts that call for flaming.

Whiskey

Whiskies are distilled from a fermented mash of grain (usually corn, rye, barley, or wheat), and then aged in oak barrels. In this country, whiskey must be distilled at less than 190 proof (although whiskey with a special designation such as bourbon, rye, etc., cannot be distilled above 160 proof) and must be bottled at no less than 80 proof.

Whiskey, when placed in barrels to age, is a clear liquid. It is during the aging period that whiskey obtains its characteristic amber color, flavor, and aroma.

The major whiskey producing countries are the United States, Canada, Scotland, and Ireland. Special grain characteristics, recipes, and distillation processes make the whiskey of each country distinct from that of the others.

American Whiskey—Although American whiskies fall into three major categories, straight whiskey, light whiskey, and blended whiskey, the United States government acknowledges thirty-three distinct types of whiskey. Only the major types (98 percent of the nation's consumption) are covered here.

Straight Whiskey is distilled from corn, rye, barley or wheat (not blended with neutral grain spirits or any other whiskey) and aged in charred oak barrels for a minimum of two years. There are four major types of straight whiskey:

1. Bourbon Whiskey is distilled from a mash of grain containing not less than 51 percent corn and is normally aged four years in new charred oak barrels. Bourbon is amber in color and full-bodied in flavor. When distilled in Kentucky it is usually referred to as Kentucky Straight Bourbon Whiskey. Bourbon is named for Bourbon County in Kentucky where this type of whiskey originated. Bourbon is also produced in Illinois, Indiana, Ohio, Pennsylvania, Tennessee, and Missouri.

2. Rye Whiskey is distilled from a mash of grain containing not less that 51 percent rye and is much like bourbon in color, but is different in taste and heavier in flavor.

3. Corn Whiskey is distilled from a mash of grain containing not less than 80 percent corn. Corn whiskey is commonly aged in re-used charred oak barrels.

4. Bottled-in-Bond Whiskey is straight whiskey, usually bourbon or rye, which is produced under United States government supervision. Though the government does not guarantee the quality of bonded whiskey, it does require that the whiskey be at least four years old, that it be bottled at 100 proof, that it be produced in one distillery by the same distiller, and that it be stored and bottled at a bonded warehouse under government supervision.

Blended Whiskey is a blend of one or more straight whiskies and neutral grain spirits containing at least 20 percent or more straight whiskey bottled at not less than 80 proof.

A blend of straight whiskies occurs when two or more straight whiskies are blended together, to the exclusion of neutral grain spirits.

Canadian Whisky—Canadian whiskies are blended whiskies, usually distilled from rye, corn, and barley. Produced only in Canada, under government supervision, most of the Canadian whisky sold in this country is at least four years old. Canadian whisky, usually lighter-bodied than American whiskey, is usually sold at 80 proof.

Scotch Whisky—Produced only in Scotland, Scotch whiskies are blended whiskies deriving their individual personalities from native barley grain and traditional pot stills. All Scotch blends contain malt whisky and grain whisky (similar to American grain neutral spirits). Scotch's distinctive smokey flavor comes from drying malted barley over peat fires. All the Scotch imported in this country is at least four years old and is usually 80 or 86 proof. Scotch sold in the rest of the world is almost always 80 proof.

Scotch-on-the-rocks

Irish Whisky—Produced only in Ireland, Irish whisky, like Scotch, is a blended whisky containing both barley malt whiskies and grain whiskies. Unlike Scotch, however, the malt is dried in coal-fired kilns and the aroma of the fires does not reach the malt. Irish whisky is heavier and more full-bodied than Scotch and is usually 86 proof.

Age is often believed to be the only indication of quality, but a whiskey, rum, or brandy can be aged too long as well as not long enough. Other factors affecting quality include variables in the distilling process itself, the types of grain used, the warehousing techniques employed, the rate of aging, and the degree of skill used in determining product maturity. Aging may make good whiskey better, but no amount of aging can make good whiskey out of bad.

Grain Neutral Spirits is a practically tasteless, colorless alcohol distilled from grain (like whiskey) but at 190 proof or above, whereas whiskey must be distilled at less than 190 proof. Used in blended whiskies, in making gin and vodkas, and in many other liquors.

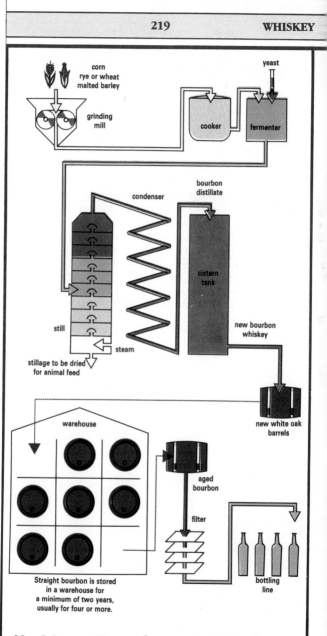

II. How Bourbon Is Made

Vodka

Vodka has humility. Colorless, tasteless, odorless it will graciously assume the characteristics of whatever it is mixed with.

The higher the proof the less flavor, and vodka is also filtered through charcoal to remove any remaining hint of flavor. There are vodkas that are specially flavored with lemon, lime, mint, and even one flavored with buffalo grass.

Vodka is made from pure grain neutral spirits distilled from fermented corn, rye, or wheat. Russian vodka used to be made from potato mash in the days of the Czars. Today it's made with grain.

Taken straight, vodka makes a fine aperitif with smoked salmon or hot sausage.

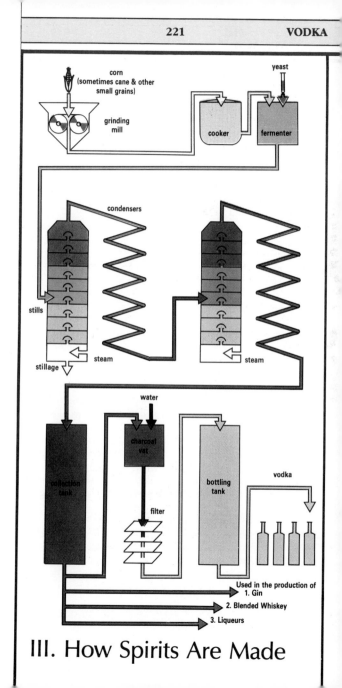

III. How Spirits Are Made

BEER

"Beer" refers to all brewed and fermented beverages that are made from malted grains and hops.

There are five major types of beer: Lager, ale, stout, porter, and bock. For all of these the 22 stages of brewing are similar. The difference between light and dark beers comes from the amount of roasting, or "kilning," of the barley malt. The more roasting, the darker the color and the greater the caramelization of malt sugars.

Usually made from barley, beer begins with germination of the grain. Once germinated, the barley is called "malt."

The malt is next dried in a hot kiln. The temperature and duration of roasting determines both the color and sweetness of the final product. The longer the roast, the darker and sweeter the beer.

Next, the roasted malt is mixed with other cereals and water and cooked.

The type of water used for beer is important. Some waters make good beers. Other waters possess minerals or tastes more suitable for ale. That's why certain areas are noted for beer or ale but seldom produce both.

After cooking, liquid from this pre-alcoholic porridge is drained off. The liquid is call "wort." It's put into a brew kettle and infused with hops, a small, soft pine cone-looking flower, which adds a depth of flowery flavor and a tang to beer.

After a few hours of boiling in the wort the hops are strained out, the wort is cooled, and yeast is added which "attacks" the malt sugar causing fermentation.

Yeast converts wort to beer. The pedigree of the yeast, the secret formula so carefully perpetuated so that the beer will have the same flavor year after year, is the brewmaster's "magic wand."

Two different types of yeasts make all the differences among beers. When "bottom" yeast finishes eating the sugar it settles to the bottom of the tank. Lager is a "bottom fermented" beer. Practically all beers brewed in the United States are lagers.

Ale, on the other hand, is a "top" fermented beverage. "Top" yeast floats on the top of the tank when it finishes with the sugar.

You can taste the difference the two yeasts make. Ale is sharper and stronger than lager, with a more pronounced flavor of hops.

The ideal serving temperature is 45°F for beer and 50°F for ale. Beer goes flat if it's served too cold. Imported beers should be served at 50°F and English or Irish stout at 55°F.

Store bottled or canned beer in a cool dark place. Extremely sensitive to sunlight, bottled beer must never be put in windows or it will acquire a "skunky" odor. At home, store cans or bottles in the lowest, coolest part of the refrigerator; not in the door shelf because jostling and drafts of warm air from the kitchen will deterioriate the beer.

To serve beer, pour it so that the stream flows directly to the center of the glass, which should be stationary on the table. This produces a nice foam or "head." Beer naturally accompanies hamburger, stew, sausage, cold cuts, lobster, and sharp cheeses.

Here are some definitions:

Beer—a generic term for all brewed and fermented beverages made from cereal grains.

Lager—bright, clear-bodied beer, effervescent. A "bottom fermented" brew.

Ale—aromatic malt brew usually fuller-bodied and more bitter than pilsner. A "top fermented" brew.

Stout—a very dark ale, sweet and strong with a pronounced hops taste.

Porter—a type of ale with a rich, heavy foam. Sweeter than ale. Not quite as strong as stout.

Pilsner—a term put on labels of light beers around the world. These are bright, lagered beers, but none equal to their marvelous namesake: the unique Pilsner Urquell from Pilsner, Bohemia.

Bock Beer—darker, sweeter, and heavier than typical beers. Made for six weeks in the spring from residue left in the vats before they are cleaned. After Prohibition was repealed in December, 1933, bars proclaimed the good news with signs that celebrated "Bock is back!"

Malt Liquor—a beer with considerable variation from light to dark color, and from a strong, hoppy flavor to little. Higher alcoholic content than most other beers.

Sweet Beer—a combination of fruit juice and beer. Yields a sweeter drink and higher alcoholic content than lagers.

Sake—actually a type of beer in that it is a re-fermented rice brew of high alcoholic content.

Light Beer—pilsners, lower in alcohol and calories, mild in taste.

Low Alcohol Beer—similar to Light Beer, but contains even less alcohol and calories.

WINE

Wine, one of the oldest beverages created for the pleasure of man, is a natural product made from grapes. Its probable Mediterranean origin predates written history, with the earliest known documents stating that wine has been made since 4000 B.C. Wine, wine-making, and the cultivation of wine grapes gradually spread throughout the civilized world via tradesmen, religious sects, and conquering armies. Today, almost every continent can enjoy wine from its own resources.

For many people, wine is an integral part of life. It enhances the enjoyment of nearly every occasion and has the capability of turning an ordinary moment into a golden memory.

But where to start? The world of wine can be overwhelming. The variety of labels seems endless, the terminology is confusing, and the customs related to serving it are varied and often mystifying.

Wine needs to be appreciated. Each wine has its own personality. Nature guarantees it will never have quite the same character each year, even considering the exact same vineyard, wine-maker, and process. This factor, combined with the ever-changing character of wine as it ages, results in a complex beverage that can satisfy tastes and temperaments all over the world.

Wine Appreciation

There are two things required to become a wine connoisseur: taste buds and a good memory. The more wines you experience, the better you'll be able to discriminate between what you do and don't like. Learning to assess quality in wine is fun and can save you money. A $12.00 bottle may not be twice as good as a $6.00 bottle, but only your palate can make that decision.

Preferences in wine are subjective and everyone's taste differs. Through the years certain guidelines have evolved, to maximize the enjoyment of wine.

Wine Tasting

There are three criteria for judging wine: color, aroma, and taste. You must first examine the wine in a clear glass for color. The deeper the color, the fuller the flavor. The wine should be clear and appealing. Murkiness indicates something has happened to change the taste and quality of the wine.

Next, swirl the glass to aerate the wine. This helps release the bouquet or aroma. Two-thirds of your judgment of wine is based on the aroma. In a light white wine, a flowery, grapey perfume may arise. The big red wines usually have a "spicy" berry character and need five to ten minutes in the glass to develop their bouquet.

Now, taste it. Take a little wine in the mouth and "whistle" the wine in to release its full flavors. Notice the components. Is it dry or sweet? Is it fruity, oaky, acidic? Is it too heavy, too light or well-balanced? And most important—do you like it?

From start to finish this procedure should take about twelve seconds.

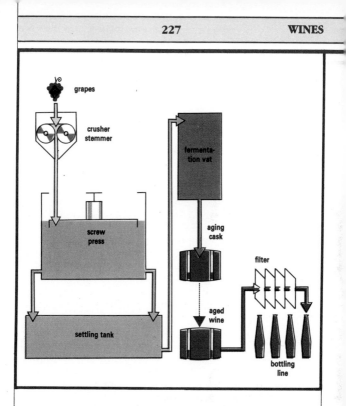

IV. How Wines are Made

Wine Production: Grapes are picked from September to October depending on variety, and put into a crusher-stemmer which removes the stems and produces grape "must". Must is pumped to a press to separate juice from the skins. (For red wine, skins are left on during fermentation.) The juice is pumped to a settling tank, then into a fermentation vat where wine yeast is added. When fermentation is complete (two to three weeks), the wine is racked several times and placed in casks for aging, if desired. After aging, wine is filtered and bottled.

Wine Service

When serving wine, there are a few basics to remember: White wine is served before red, light wine before heavy, and dry before sweet. Red wines should be served at room temperature (65°) or slightly cool to the touch. White wines, rosés, and light reds such as Beaujolais are best served with a slight chill. For maximum effervescense, Champagne and sparkling wine are best served very cold (45°) but not so chilled that the delicate flavors are lost.

For each wine type there is a proper kind of glass that provides optimum enjoyment. The best all-purpose glass for both red and white wine is an eight-to-ten-ounce clear glass that has a large bowl at the base and is slightly tapered inward on the top. The bowl allows plenty of room for swirling and the tapered top directs the aroma. For Champagne, a tall, clear flute-shaped glass, preferably crystal, ensures that the wine will retain the long stream of bubbles the wine-maker went to such great effort to offer you. Shallow, bowl-shaped glasses give the wine a broad surface area from which the bubbles dissipate rapidly and cause the wine to go flat.

It is common to have more than one glass at a table setting. The type of wine and wineglasses will depend on the meal prepared.

Wine and Food

It is important to consider how a dish is prepared in deciding what wine would best complement it. In general, wines produced in a certain region tend to go well with dishes from the same region. For instance, Chianti is well-matched with full-flavored Italian cuisine and French red Burgundies with hearty stews and roasts.

Food & Wine Chart

Sparkling wine and Champagne—Aperitifs, wild game, caviar, oysters, roasted almonds, fresh fruit.

Dry white wine—Seafood, shellfish, domestic fowl, veal, cream sauces, mild cheeses, light dishes.

Rosé wine—Baked ham, turkey, sausages, pork.

Medium-bodied red wine—Lamb, pork, wild game, charred fish or fowl, pâté, mild blue cheeses.

Full-bodied red wine—Roast beef, steak, charred red meats, fuller dishes, mild to slightly sharp cheeses.

Sweet (dessert) wine—Foie gras, fruits, pastry, and simple desserts.

Dry Sherry/Dry Madiera—Aperitifs, soups.

Port and Sweet Sherry—After dinner, cheeses.

Wine Storage

All wines should be stored in a cool, dry place. Each should be kept on its side so that the cork remains moist. If the cork dries out, air will enter the bottle and oxidize the wine. Once opened, keep the leftover wine corked tightly and place in the refrigerator. Most wines will keep like this for only a few days. After that, the wine absorbs oxygen and turns to vinegar. If your wine has "turned," add some olive oil and Dijon-type mustard. It's an excellent dressing and you may decide to forgive wine's volatile nature. A second alternative for leftover wine is to decant into smaller bottles. The fuller the bottle, the less likely it will spoil since the contact with air is kept to a minimum.

If wine, particularly red wine, has been stored for a number of years, a sediment may form on the side of the bottle. This is a natural side effect of aging and does not mean the wine has spoiled. However, when serving, first decant the wine, making sure that the sediment is not disturbed. The wine should be smooth and velvety.

A Glossary of Basic Wine Terms

Acidity—A term used to indicate tartness or sharpness to the taste due to the presence of fruit acids.

Aroma—That portion of the wine's odor derived from the grape variety and fermentation.

Balance—A tasting term denoting complete harmony among the main components of a wine.

Body—The weight or fullness of wine on the palate.

Bouquet—That portion of a wine's odor which develops after it is bottled.

Cooperage—Containers used for holding or ageing wine before being bottled. They may be made out of stainless steel, oak or other wood.

Dry—A tasting term to denote the absence of sweetness in wine.

Enology—The study of wine-making.

Fermentation—The process of converting natural grape sugar into alcohol and carbon dioxide by the addition of yeast.

Generic Wine—Wine blended with several grape varieties in which the character of any one variety does not dominate. These wines are labeled with a generalized term such as chablis, burgundy, or rhine.

Nose—The total odor of wine composed of aroma, bouquet and other factors.

Residual Sugar—The natural grape sugar that is left in a wine which determines the sweetness level.

Tannin—The components in a wine that have an astringent, puckery and sometimes bitter quality, and a mouth-drying aftertaste.

Varietal Wine—Wine made from one grape variety.

Vintage Wine—Wine made from grapes that are harvested in one given year.

Chilled Shadow Creek Wine

Wines of the United States

Although California, New York, Oregon, and Washington are the chief wine-producing states in America, several other states such as Virginia and Texas produce small quantities of wine. This is partly due to the skilled young American wine-makers who have emerged from the University of California at Davis, the famed United States School of Enology (wine-making). Their new scientific methods, coupled with the experience and tradition of European wine-making, account for a thriving new wine industry in America as well as many international awards for wines of excellence.

The East

The most important eastern wine-producing state is New York. The wines of New York are dissimilar to the wines of California and Europe because of the different grape species used for wine production. Instead of the traditional European grape varieties, the grapes used are either native American varieties such as Concord, Isabella, Catawba, and Delaware, or are the hybrids such as Baco and Seyvel Blanc. These grape varieties produce wines distinctively different from those made from European grape varieties but the wines at best are extremely good.

The West

Oregon and Washington are extremely important wine-producing states; however, California out-produces them by far. The production of wine has a long history in California dating back to the early Spanish missions, yet wine as a commercial product is a relatively new venture. In the early 1960s California had only a handful of wineries. Now over 575 wineries exist, and more are opening each year.

The principal grape varieties used in California are the same classic varieties used in France and Germany. Yet, instead of identifying the wine by where the vineyard is located as is done in Europe, the wine is identified by the grape variety. The reason for this is that any one grape variety can flourish in several geographic districts and any one district can produce good grapes of several different varieties.

A wine label from California is very easy to read. United States law requires that wine labels specify the producer or brand name, wine type (grapes used or blend), the region of origin, the bottler, the alcoholic content, and the year of harvest. Behind each one of these titles are specific requirements the wine must meet before being released to the public. This ensures quality control.

There are many grape growing regions in California from north of San Francisco down to San Diego. The major fine wine-producing areas are Napa, Sonoma, Mendocino, Monterey, and the Central Coast. Each region has characteristics different from the other due to dissimilar climate, soil, and topography. Within these regions are smaller areas with unique microclimates that produce wines that have singular qualities unlike those of the surrounding area. Thus one grape variety can do well in many regions and produce completely different results.

All regions in California produce a wide selection of wine types. In each region there are particular varieties they are noted for.

Region	Grape Varieties
Napa	Chardonnay, Sauvignon Blanc, Cabernet Sauvignon, Merlot
Mendocino/ Sonoma	Chardonnay, Sauvignon Blanc, Cabernet Sauvignon, Zinfandel, Sparkling wine
Monterey	Chardonnay, Johannisberg Riesling
Central Coast	Chardonnay, Sauvignon Blanc, Johannisberg Riesling, Pinot Noir

Most wineries permit tours of their facilities and tasting of their recently released wines. The people are friendly and the countryside is beautiful. It's an excellent excuse to visit California.

Wines of France

Without France the wine world would never be where it is today. Fortunately for us, since 500 B.C. France has continued to perfect grape growing and wine-making techniques. It not only produces most of the important wine types in the world but also many of the greatest wines.

One of the reasons for the excellence of French wines is a set of official guidelines for wine production. Under a law called the *Appellation d'Origine Contrôllée,* the production of each vineyard is held to high standards of quality. Only wines of particular varietals, produced within carefully drawn boundaries, and under certain processes may be labeled with the name of the vineyard.

For example, Champagne refers only to sparkling wines made within the Champagne district of France. Sparkling wines produced outside of this district—even if using the same grape varieties and wine-making procedure—are merely referred to as *vin mousseux* or sparkling wine.

There are several extremely important wine districts in France that produce very different wines. The most notable are presented in the following section.

Bordeaux

Bordeaux is actually a city in southwest France surrounded by vineyards. It is mainly known for its red wines but their dry and sweet white wines are among the finest made. Within Bordeaux are several sub-districts that use similar grape varieties yet produce wines of different character. The primary grape varieties are Cabernet Sauvignon, Cabernet Franc, and Merlot. Red wines that are medium–full bodied, fragrant, and complex come from these regions: St. Estèphe, Pauillac, St. Julien, Médoc, Margaux, and Graves. Red wines that are full bodied, heavy, and rich come from St. Émilion and Pomerol.

Red Bordeaux Vintage Chart:

Great Years: 45, 49, 53, 59, 61, 70, 75, 82

Good Years: 55, 62, 64, 66, 71, 73, 76, 78, 79, 80, 81

Graves also produces austere dry whites from the grape varieties Sauvignon Blanc and Sémillion. Other white wine areas are Sauternes and Barsac. Both use the same grape varieties as the white Graves but the grapes ae harvested overripe. These sweet wines are golden in color with the rich flavor of ripe pears and apricots.

White Bordeaux (Sauternes) Vintage Chart:

Great Years: 45, 47, 49, 50, 55, 59, 62, 67, 71

Good Years: 53, 57, 61, 62, 66, 70, 75, 76, 79

Burgundy

Located in eastern France, Burgundy is divided into five main districts each very different from the others. The wines are made either by the vineyard owner or by *negociants* who buy wines from the various growers, blend them together and sell the final product from their particular firm. In purchasing a bottle of Burgundy, it is just as important to know the reputation of the producer or *negociant* as it is to know the reputation of the vineyard. The five main districts of Burgundy are:

Chablis—Producing excellent austere white wines from the grape varietal Chardonnay. These fresh, flinty dry wines are best matched with delicate seafoods and shellfish.

Maconnais—Producing popular, light dry wines primarily from Chardonnay grapes. The most well-known wines are: Macon-Villages, Pouilly-Fuissé, and St.-Véran.

Chalonnais—Producing light dry reds and dry whites.

Beaujolais—Producing light fruity red wines from the Gamay grape variety. One of most widely drunk red wines in the world and attractively priced.

Côte d'Or—Within this region are two subregions—the Côte de Nuits (north) and the Côte de Beaune (south). The Côte de Nuits is responsible for the greatest red Burgundies, such as Chambertin, Vosne-Romanée, Vougeot, Musigny, and Nuits St.-Georges. These wines are made from Pinot Noir grapes and in character are generally medium–full bodied, fragrant, and wonderfully complex.

The other subregion, Côte de Beaune, is responsible for the greatest white Burgundies such as Meursault, Chassagne-Montrachet, Puligny Montrachet, and most importantly, Le Montrachet. The wines are made from the Chardonnay grape varietal and in character are generally medium–full bodied, rich, and buttery.

Burgundy Vintage Chart:

Great Years: 61, 62, 64, 66, 69, 71, 76, 78, 81

Good Years: 67, 70, 72, 73, 79, 80

Champagne
Thanks to the discoveries of the seventeenth-century monk, Dom Perignon, sparkling wines are enjoyed the world over. Champagne is made by a costly time-consuming process called *méthode champenoise*. Essentially, this is the process by which still wine is made sparkling by allowing it to ferment a second time in the bottle thus producing the characteristic bubbles in champagne. There are other

ways to make a wine sparkling but this produces the finest results and is the only process allowed in Champagne.

The still base wine or *cuvée* must be near flawless. For the base, Chardonnay or Pinot Noir grape varieties are used singularly or in a blend. If the label says "Blanc de Noir," the wine is made entirely from Pinot Noir. If the term "Blanc de Blanc" is used, the wine is 100% Chardonnay. Most wines are a blend of both varieties.

Even though Champagne is produced only in good years, the finest wines are both vintage-dated and non-vintage-dated. The initial wine blend is more important than the year. Champagne, at best, is a versatile elegant beverage with toasty, lemony flavors. Each wine is labeled according to its sweetness level.

Term	Characteristic
Natural	Bone dry
Brut	Dry
Extra Sec (Extra Dry)	Fairly dry
Sec	Slightly sweet
Demi-Sec	Fairly sweet
Doux	Sweet

Rhone

The vineyards of Rhone are located in southern France on steep, sun-drenched granite cliffs. This area produces wines that are deep in color, very hearty, and big. Most of the finer Rhone wines are pressed from one kind of grape, sometimes two or three—with the exception of Chateauneuf-du-Pape, in which thirteen grapes are allowed. The principal red grape varieties are Syrah and Grenache. The principal white variety is Voignier. Important areas of Rhone include Côte Rotie, Hermitage, Chateauneuf-du-Pape, and St. Joseph. Currently the best buys are the inexpensive red and white Côte du Rhones.

Loire Valley

Although there is almost no wine sold under the label Loire, there are a number of well-known vineyard areas along the river including Vouvray, Sancerre, Pouilly, and Muscadet.

Vouvray—Perhaps the best-known district. Made from Chenin Blanc grapes, the wines are light and delicately fruity with a hint of sweetness. A substantial amount of sparkling and some semi-sparkling wines are also made.

Sancerre and *Pouilly-sur-Loire*—Both primarily produce dry white wines from the grape varietal Sauvignon Blanc. The wines have a strong varietal character and at best are excellent.

Muscadet—Produces delightful light dry white wines with a crisp finish. The wines are made from the grape variety Melon of Burgundy.

Alsace—French Rhine Wines

Located in northeast France, Alsace borders Germany and, in fact, produces white wines with Germanic characteristics. The finest wines are fairly dry and made from the varieties White Riesling and Gewürztraminer. Gewürztraminer is the most unique tasting white wine in France. It has a very flowery aroma and an exotic spicy flavor.

Alsace is also known for its *eaux-de-vie*. These are fruit brandies made from cherries (kirsch), wild strawberries (fraise), raspberries (framboise), plum (mirabelle), as well as other fruits.

Wines of Germany

Germany's vineyards lie as far north as grapes can ripen. The vineyards are located on steep hillsides with the best vines facing south for maximum exposure to the sun. Due to difficult location and weather, the wines are expensive but worth the price.

Most of the wines of Germany are white and range from sweet to sweeter to sweetest. However, it's hard to know what you are getting if you can't decipher a German wine label. Once you can do that, you can buy a German wine with complete confidence. Of the world's wine labels, the German gives the most precise and complete information about the wine within.

The label tells you which of the three types you are buying:

A) *Tafelwein* (Table Wine)
Wine for everyday consumption. This wine is infrequently imported.

B) *Qualitätswein* (Quality Wine)
A higher quality than Tafelwein.

C) *Qualitätswein mit Prädikat* (Quality Wine with Special Attributes)
The highest quality category. Wines must be made from White Riesling grapes. The Pradikats or special attributes refer to five levels of ripeness and sweetness.

1) *Kabinett*—(1–5% residual sugar) Slightly sweet dinner fare.

2) *Spätlese*—(6–12% residual sugar) Late picked. Fairly sweet.

3) *Auslese*—(12–18% residual sugar) Selected late picked. Very sweet.

4) *Beerenauslese*—(20–30% residual sugar) Very sweet. Berry-selected, late picked.

5) *Trockenbeerenauslese*—(30% or more residual sugar) Extremely sweet. Dried berry-selected, late picked.

A) *Eiswein*—wine from grapes picked and crushed frozen. Very sweet.

At the very top of the label is the name of the growing region. Just under that is the year of harvest.

In bold type across the wine label are the town and vineyards that produced the wine. An *er* suffix is placed on a village name so a wine from the town Bernkastel becomes Bernkast*ler* on the bottle.

Just under the town name you'll see the grape variety. The most important varieties are Johannesberg (White) Riesling, Sylvaner and Müller-Thurgau. The label then tells if the wine is dry (trocken) or semi-dry (Halbtrocken).

The last two lines, which look like fine print on a contract, tell the ripeness of the grapes at harvest, the official passed-quality-control number, and whether or not the wine was estate-bottled or produced by a cooperative of growers.

There are eleven wine districts in Germany. They are: Nahe, Franconia (Franken), Baden and Württemburg, Ahr, Rheinhessen, Palatinate (Pfalz), Rheingau, Middle Rhine, Mosel (with Saar and Ruwer), and Bergstrasse. The two most important districts are the Mosel-Saar-Ruwer producing stylish elegant wines with "steely aristocracy" and the Rheingau producing fuller, more lush wines than the Mosel with ripe, apricot fruit.

German Vintage Chart:

Great Years: 53, 59, 71, 75, 76, 83

Good Years: 64, 66, 69, 70, 73, 79

Wines of Italy

In the past, Italian wines have suffered not only from the haphazard methods of wine-making and growing but also from an easygoing attitude concerning nomenclature. The root of the trouble was the government's failure to safeguard place names of the fine wine regions. The French government, afraid of having its market flooded with cheap Italian wines, urged the Italian government to set up control laws somewhat along the same lines of their Appellation d'Origine Contrôlle.

In July 1963 regulations for controlling place names, or Denomination of Origin (D.O.C.), were made law. The best quality, government guaranteed standards, are labeled *Denominazione di Origine Controllata e Garantita* which means the location of the vineyards are "controlled and guaranteed" to be of consistently high quality. Today, Italy is the largest producer and exporter of fine wine in the world.

There are some 18 distinct wine-growing regions in Italy located throughout the country. The most well known are: *Piedmont*—producing Barolo, Barbaresco, Gattinara, Barbera, Asti Spumante, and others; *Tuscany*—producing Chianti and Brunello di Montalcino; *Veneto*—producing Soave, Bardolino, Valpolicella; *Latium*—producing Frascati.

Popular Italian Wines

Amarone—Red wines made from grapes that are dried, like raisins, to concentrate sugar and increase alcoholic content (up to 15%). Heavy flavor.

Asti Spumante—Muscat grapes go into this sparkling white wine that's grapey and sweet. Very popular in Italy and growing in popularity in the United States.

Torre dei Conti Asti Spumante

Barbaresco—A rough tannic red wine from Nebbiolo grapes. One of the best produced; better and smoother when aged.

Barbera d'Alba—Fruity red wine with high tannic overtones.

Barbera d'Asti—"More refined" relative of the wine above; should be aged 4–8 years.

Bardolino—Light red table wine.

Barolo—The "king" of Italian wines. A strong wine having a perfume that's the "muscleman" of Piedmont reds. However, the wine is velvety smooth when aged.

Chianti—Medium–light bodied, sometimes flinty red wines. Very aromatic. Serve with grilled meats and fowl. Made from Sangiovese grapes (about 70%) and the rest a blend of up to five other varieties.

Chianti Classico—Aged and elegant Chianti.

Frascati—Fruity, dry young white wines.

Gattinara—Like a Barolo but more refined. Hearty and full-flavored.

Grappa—Fiery grape brandy made from the last of the pressed grape pulp. Smells and tastes like wood alcohol.

Grignolino—Rose or light red wine with ample bouquet and a little "kick."

Lambrusco—Light, lively red. Serve chilled.

Marsala—Dark, sugar-fortified dessert wine from Sicily. Used often to create Veal Marsala and a custard-like dessert called *zabaglione.*

Orvieto—Fruity dry light wines.

Pinot Grigio—A little fruitier than most Italian whites. Dry.

Soave—Popular light dry white wine made in the town of Soave near Verona. Drink young.

Spanna—Another name for the Nebbiolo grape and a red wine produced from it in Piedmont. Rich, full flavor.

Valpolicella—Light red wine, good slightly chilled. Soft. Ruby-colored. The Italian equivalent of Beaujolais.

Verdicchio—Light, crisp, dry white wine. Pale green.

Wines of Spain

Spain has more vineyards than any other country in Europe but lower yields than Italy and France. This is partly due to eclectic ideas of what constitutes a vineyard and partly reflects the haphazard nature of much of Spain's wine industry. Currently, there is an expansion of grape growing and the gradual utilization of modern wine-making methods.

The wine regions of Spain tend to be casually defined. The main quality regions are Jerez, Rioja, and Catalonia.

Rioja, located in northern Spain, is known for its red table wines. These are made in the style of French Bordeaux and aged in oak at least two years. The result is a smooth, dry red with flavor, aromatic bouquet and a warm aftertaste of oak. Spanish wines more than other world wines rely on oak aging which results in mellower, warmer flavors.

In northeast Spain, *Catalonia* produces a wide variety of inexpensive wines but is best known in the United States for its sparkling wine. The sparkling wines of Penedés are very good producing well-made dry sparklers with definite flavors.

Spain is best-known for its sherry and *Jerez de la Frontera* is the center of sherry country. The chalky soil there adds special characteristics and fineness to the wine.

Sherry is a fortified wine to which grape brandy has been added to increase the alcoholic content. The Palomino grape is primarily used with the grape variety Pedro Ximenez kept for the sweetest wines.

Sherry is not known by vineyard or vintage. The vintage is lost in the "Solera" system. This system helps keep the same quality and character of the sherry over the years and constantly refreshes the fino types. This progressive system employs a series of casks graduated by age ranging from fine old sherry to fresh youthful sherry. When ready to bottle, a portion of the oldest sherry leaves the cask or "butt." An equal quantity is drawn from the next oldest sherry butt and replaces the wine in the oldest butt. Then, to replace the wine lost in the second-oldest sherry butt, an equal quantity is drawn from the next older butt—and so on. The sherry is essentially "ageless."

Types of Sherry

Fino—A pale light gold wine in which "flor," a wine-yeast, develops on top during production, adding character. The wine is very dry, has a fresh appley nose and delicate flavors. To be drunk young.

Manzanilla—This is both a fino wine and a wine in its own right. Produced near the sea, the salt air affects the flavor giving a special tang. A fresh light tart wine.

Amontillado—A softer, darker-colored sherry than fino. The best Amontillados are old finos with nutty powerful flavor and usually slightly sweet.

Oloroso—This sherry is fuller in body than the Amontillado. The wine is strong, nutty, and pungent. It is the basis for the best sweet sherries, often known as milk or cream.

Wines of Portugal

There are regions in Portugal that make table wines, such as Dao, which produces wines similar to the Riojas of Spain. But Portugal's main claim to fame is Port and Madeira.

Madeira

Madeira, an island located off the coast of Morocco, is considered to be a part of Portugal. Wine has been a major product there for over 400 years. Fame came once Madeira was made suitable for export by being fortified by brandy, and the long sea voyages through tropical heat speeded up the long maturing process, resulting in the caramel tang by which all Madeiras can now be recognized.

Today, the wines are "baked" to achieve this tang, and the shippers of Madeira use the Spanish solera system to blend their wine into consistent brands.

There are four distinct types of Madeira named after the grapes from which they are produced, ranging in levels of sweetness. From dry to sweet they are: Sercial, Verdelho, Bual (Boal), and Malmsey. Rainwater is a blend and may be dry or medium sweet.

Port

Port's name was derived from the city from where it was shipped at the mouth of the Douro, Oporto. A blend of many grape varieties, the wine is made by running off partially fermented red wine into a barrel a quarter full of brandy while the wine still has half of its grape sugar. The brandy stops the fermentation so that the wine is strong and sweet.

When completed the wine is a deep opaque purple, rich in fruit, tannic acid, and long lived. There are several types of port.

Vintage Port—This is among the world's best wines. Not produced every year, the wine is made entirely from one exceptional year and bottled early for laying away and ageing.

Vintage Port Vintage Chart:

Best Years: 45, 47, 48, 50, 55, 58, 60, 63, 66, 67, 70, 75, 77, 80

Crusted Port—Good wine handled as is a Vintage Port but not necessarily of one vintage.

Tawny Port—Port aged many years in oak producing a tawny color. Very fine quality and smooth.

Ruby Port—Young port aged in wood a relatively short period of time. Deep in color, fruity but rough.

Late-Bottled Vintage Port—Wine of a good year kept much longer in wood than Vintage Port. A lighter wine.

White Port—Port made from white grapes.

MEASUREMENTS

A Buying Guide

Use the following as a reference for determining approximately how many bottles you may need for various occasions.

For Cocktails	You'll Need at Least	For Buffet or Dinner	You'll Need at Least	For an After-Dinner Party	You'll Need at Least
10 to 16 drinks	1-750 ml	8 cocktails 8 glasses wine 4 liqueurs 8 highballs	1-750 ml 2 bottles 1-500 ml 1-750 ml	12 to 16 drinks	1-750 ml for 4 people
15 to 22 drinks	2-750 mls	12 cocktails 12 glasses wine 8 liqueurs 18 highballs	1-750 ml 2 bottles 1-750 ml 2-750 mls	18 to 26 drinks	2-750 mls for 6 people
18 to 24 drinks	2-750 mls	16 cocktails 16 glasses wine 10 liqueurs 18 highballs	1-750 ml 3 bottles 1-750 ml 2-750 mls	20 to 34 drinks	2-750 mls for 8 people
20 to 40 drinks	3-750 mls	24 cocktails 24 glasses wine 16 liqueurs 30 highballs	2-750 mls 4 bottles 1-750 ml 3-750 mls	25 to 45 drinks	3-750 mls for 12 people
40 to 65 drinks	4-750 mls	40 cocktails 40 glasses wine 25 liqueurs 50 highballs	3-750 mls 7 bottles 2-750 mls 4-750 mls	45 to 75 drinks	5-750 mls for 20 people

Measuring

Even the most professional bartender measures the ingredients of every drink, even though experience may permit some to do this by eye and by skillful freehand pouring. However, to make a perfect drink every time, measure all ingredients. Remember, too, that many drinks can be spoiled by being too strong as well as too weak.

Some standard bar measures:

1 Dash (or splash) .... 1/6 teaspoon (1/32 ounce)
1 Teaspoon (bar spoon) .... 1/8 ounce
1 Tablespoon .... 3/8 ounce
1 Pony .... 1 ounce
1 Jigger (barglass) .... $1^1/_2$ ounces
1 Wineglass .... 4 ounces
1 Split .... 6 ounces
1 Cup .... 8 ounces

Metric Standards of Fill for Distilled Spirits

Metric Size	Fluid Ounces	Nearest U.S. Equivalent	Fluid Ounces	Number of Bottles per Case
50 ml.	1.7	miniature	1.6	120
100 ml.	3.4	1/4 pint	4	48
200 ml.	6.8	1/2 pint	8	48
375 ml.	12.7	3/4 pint	12	24
500 ml.	16.9	1 pint	16	24
750 ml.	25.4	4/5 quart	25.6	12
1 liter	33.8	1 quart	32	12
1.75 liters	59.2	1/2 gallon	64	6

Metric Sizes for Wine

Name of Package	New Metric Size	Equivalent Fluid Oz.	Bottles Per Case
Split	187 ml.	6.34	48
Tenth	375 ml.	12.68	24
Fifth	750 ml.	25.36	12
Quart	1 liter	33.81	12
Magnum	1.5 liters	50.72	6
Jeroboam	3 liters	101.44	4

ml. = milliliters   1 liter = 1,000 milliliters

Liquid Measures

Metric Units

10 milliliters	= 1 centiliter
10 centiliters	= 1 deciliter
10 deciliters	= 1 liter
10 liters	= 1 decaliter
10 decaliters	= 1 hectoliter
10 hectoliters	= 1 kiloliter

Metric and United States Equivalents

U.S. Unit	Metric Unit
1 fluid ounce	= 29.573 milliliters
1 quart	= 9.4635 deciliters 0.94635 liter
1 gallon	= 3.7854 liters
0.033814 fluid ounce	= 1 milliliter
3.3814 fluid ounces	= 1 deciliter
33.814 fluid ounces 1.0567 quarts 0.26417 gallon	= 1 liter

INDEX

If you know the name of the mixed drinks you desire, you need not use this index, all drinks are listed alphabetically throughout the book.

This index is arranged so that you may choose specific types of drinks such as cocktails, fizzes, highballs, etc., or cocktails made with gin, vodka, whiskey, or other ingredients.

HIGHBALLS

These are all-time favorites and simple to make. Any liquor may be used in combination with ice, soda, or water.

HOT DRINKS

IRISH WHISKY DRINKS

JULEPS

Native to Kentucky, juleps are cool and refreshing anywhere. Traditionally made with Kentucky bourbon and fresh mint leaves and served in a frosted glass with straws.

MARTINIS

The original martini recipe called for half
dry gin and half dry vermouth. Today,
popular proportions for an extra dry
martini range from 5-to-1 to an 8-to-1
ratio. The greater proportion of gin to
vermouth, the "drier" the martini. Always
pour the gin first then the vermouth.

MELON LIQUEUR DRINKS

MINT GIN DRINKS

NON-ALCOHOLIC DRINKS

ORANGE LIQUEUR DRINKS

ORANGE GIN DRINKS

PEACH BRANDY DRINKS

PEPPERMINT SCHNAPPS

POUSSE CAFÉS

These sweet, striped wonders are made
from a series of liqueurs poured in
succession so that one floats on top of
another. Follow the recipes exactly to get
the layers of ingredients in the right
order.

PUNCHES

Perfect for gatherings, punches can be
mixed in endless variety.

RICKEYS

A cross between a collins and a sour, rickeys are always made with lime, cracked ice, and a carbonated beverage.

ROCK AND RYE DRINKS

RUM DRINKS

SAKE DRINKS

SANGAREES

These are taller, sweet old-fashioneds without bitters.

SCOTCH

SLINGS

These are like sangarees, but made with the addition of lemon juice and a twist of lemon peel.